Using Marginal Damages in Environmental Policy

Using Marginal Damages
in Environmental Policy

A Study of Air Pollution
in the United States

Nicholas Z. Muller
Robert Mendelsohn

The AEI Press

Publisher for the American Enterprise Institute

WASHINGTON, D.C.

Distributed by arrangement with the Rowman & Littlefield Publishing Group, 4501 Forbes Boulevard, Suite 200, Lanham, Maryland 20706. To order, call toll free 1-800-462-6420 or 1-717-794-3800. For all other inquiries, please contact AEI Press, 1150 Seventeenth Street, N.W., Washington, D.C. 20036, or call 1-800-862-5801.

Library of Congress Cataloging-in-Publication Data

Muller, Nicholas Z.
  Using marginal damages in environmental policy : a study of air pollution in the United States / Nicholas Z. Muller and Robert Mendelsohn.
     pages cm
  Includes bibliographical references and index.
  ISBN 978-0-8447-7218-9 (cloth) — ISBN 0-8447-7218-6 (cloth) —
ISBN 978-0-8447-7220-2 (ebook) — ISBN 0-8447-7220-8 (ebook)
  1. Air quality management—United States. 2. Air—Pollution—Government policy—United States. 3. Air—Pollution—Economic aspects—United States. 4. Environmental policy—United States. 5. Industries—Environmental aspects—United States. 6. Damages—United States. I. Mendelsohn, Robert O., 1952- II. Title.
  TD883.2.M85 2012
  363.739'260973—dc23
                                                                2012029459

Printed in Mexico

Contents

List of Illustrations

Figures

Tables

NOTE: Unless otherwise noted, charts are derived from authors' calculations.

Introduction

In this book, we argue that the United States has the opportunity to improve its air pollution regulatory regime. It can do so by reforming its current regulations—which are a mix of command-and-control policies and cap-and-trade programs—to be more economically efficient. We provide the theoretical apparatus to demonstrate that efficient regulations should be preferred over current regulations, and we argue that we now have the data and methods to make the design of an efficient regulatory regime possible. We also show how these data can be used to begin to develop a system of environmental accounts that measure the damages associated with pollution in the United States. Efficient regulations would be the next step in the evolution of air pollution regulation in the United States, which has passed through several stages over the last six decades.

Before World War II, there was little in the way of binding environmental regulation in the United States. After World War II, state and local governments began to react to deteriorating environmental conditions by controlling emissions. The federal government's role in this area was initiated by the passage of the Clean Air Act (CAA) in 1963. The first federal regulations to control emissions were in the 1965 amendments to the CAA that established performance standards for automobile emissions. The CAA amendments of 1967 and 1969 established national emission standards for stationary sources and criteria for ambient air quality standards (USEPA 2008). The CAA amendments required the use of specific control technologies by polluters. These amendments employed technology standards.

In 1970, further amendments to the CAA created the U.S. Environmental Protection Agency (USEPA) and developed the National Ambient Air Quality Standards, which set maximum allowable concentrations of certain air pollutants harmful to human health for every county in the United States. Furthermore, the USEPA was granted broad authority to set emission standards across a range of existing pollution sources and to mandate more stringent standards for new sources. The 1970 CAA resulted in notable reductions in air pollution. Figure I-1 shows historic emission levels for three principal air pollutants: sulfur dioxide (SO_2), volatile organic compounds (VOCs), and nitrogen oxides (NO_x). This figure shows that the first appreciable emission reductions did not occur until the passage of the 1970 CAA; emissions of SO_2, NO_x, and VOCs all peaked in 1970 and declined precipitously thereafter.

Although a series of important amendments to the CAA were passed in 1977, our brief history of air pollution policy in the United States moves next to the 1990 amendments to the CAA. The 1990 amendments highlight the use of cost-effective market-based policies, which stand in stark contrast to the traditional reliance on command-and-control instruments embodied in earlier policies. The 1990 amendments established the first cost-effective regulations through the enactment of a cap-and-trade program. Under the

FIGURE I-1

HISTORIC EMISSION TRENDS IN THE UNITED STATES FOR SULFUR DIOXIDE, VOLATILE ORGANIC COMPOUNDS, AND NITROGEN OXIDES FROM 1940 TO 2007

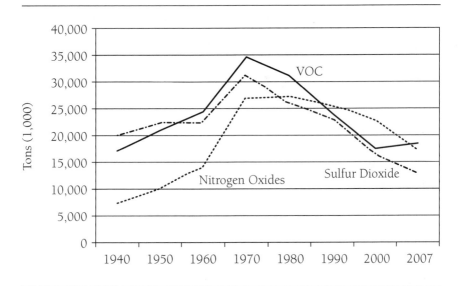

SOURCE: U.S. Environmental Protection Agency 2008.

Acid Rain Program, which was established by Title IV of the 1990 amendments, fossil fuel–powered electric generating plants were issued tradable permits for SO_2 emissions. These permits allowed firms to generate emissions of SO_2 provided that they held an allowance for each ton emitted. If any firm anticipated not having enough allowances, it could purchase additional allowances from another firm. Conversely, if a firm abated enough emissions so that it had excess permits, it was allowed to sell the permits to other firms. Recognizing that allowances are a valuable asset, regulated firms had an incentive to invest in abatement technology in order to sell their allowances to other participants in the program. This cap-and-trade program is cost-effective because each polluter equates the cost of abating an additional ton to the current permit price. The cap-and-trade program for SO_2 is estimated to have reduced abatement costs for utilities by as much as $1 billion annually. Later in the 1990s a similar cap-and-trade program for NO_x emissions was instituted in the eastern United States to control ozone levels.

Regulation under the CAA has achieved marked reductions in pollution discharges, but these programs have been costly. The USEPA estimates that society spent $523 billion cumulatively on air pollution abatement and regulatory costs between 1970 and 1990 (USEPA 1997, 1999). However, they have yielded an impressive rate of return. The cumulative benefit due to cleaner air stemming from the CAA between 1970 and 1990 is estimated to be $20 trillion (USEPA 1999).

This comparison of costs and benefits suggests that the air pollution regulations implemented in the last half of the twentieth century, taken as a whole, have been a good investment. However, this does not mean that the regulations cannot be improved. With the continued reductions of emissions stipulated in the 1990 CAA amendments, the marginal cost of abatement has grown quite high for some pollutants. As a result, regulators and scholars need to ask whether the benefits of more abatement are expected to exceed the costs. Furthermore, in order to improve the efficiency of extant regulations, society should explore whether, for certain pollutants emitted from particular sources, the regulations are too strict. Concurrently, we must determine whether, for other pollutants emitted from other places, the regulations continue to be too lax. It is important to refine current regulations to ensure that continued investments in abatement are justified.

Undertaking such analyses can improve the overall efficiency of the entire regulatory program.

While cost-effective cap-and-trade programs reduce abatement costs, these programs may also be improved. By featuring one price for all SO_2 allowances, the current trading system gives polluters an identical incentive to curtail a marginal ton of SO_2. This is problematic because the benefit of SO_2 reductions varies depending on where abatement occurs. And because efficiency requires that polluters are induced to equate their marginal cost of reducing emissions to the marginal damage of additional emissions, having one price for permits forces the system away from an efficient outcome (Montgomery 1972; Baumol and Oates 1988). Therefore, the current trading systems are not efficient. The United States can improve its current mix of cost-effective trading regimes and standards by moving toward efficiency.

Given that the case for efficient regulations is so strong and that it has been advocated by economists for so many years, why have such regulations not yet been adopted? First, it is difficult to get regulators and polluters to adopt a new approach. Change is costly, and the policy process favors the status quo. But perhaps more important, to implement an efficient regulatory regime, a regulator must be able to measure marginal damages. This requires linking emissions to final physical consequences, which is a daunting task. Moreover, in order to compare impacts to abatement costs, the impacts must be expressed in monetary terms. And although the monetary values of some air pollution impacts, such as the value of reduced crop yields, are straightforward to calculate, others are very difficult to calculate. In particular, the very act of valuing effects on health, and especially on mortality rates, is contentious. The value affixed to mortality risks, which comprise the bulk of air pollution damages, reflects a social choice. Arriving at one value for mortality risks in the evaluation of public policies is understandably difficult, given the wide range of individual values held by different members of society. Furthermore, some stakeholders find it unpleasant to consider consciously making trade-offs between money and mortality risks even though any actual policy choice implies a value for this trade-off whether the value is explicitly stated or not.

This book demonstrates that it is possible to overcome these hurdles and to estimate the marginal damages of air pollution in the United States. In fact, we provide estimates of the marginal damages of air pollution that cover the entire contiguous United States. With this information, we argue that it is possible to begin to design an efficient regulatory regime for air pollution.

The calculation relies on an integrated assessment model that links emissions to damages (see figure I-2). To calibrate this integrated assessment model requires organizing findings from a broad set of scientific disciplines, including economics, engineering, atmospheric physics and chemistry, epidemiology, toxicology, forestry, ecology, and agriculture. The model emulates the dispersion of the pollution through the atmosphere, the exposure of sensitive receptors (such as people and crops) to the pollution concentrations, and the physical damage attendant on this exposure (mortality, reduced yields, and so forth). Finally, the model assigns a monetary value to each physical outcome. This causal chain links emissions to damages measured in dollars.

Integrated assessment models are widely used both in the academic literature and by policymakers to link total emissions to total damages (Mendelsohn 1980; Nordhaus 1992; Burtraw et al. 1998; USEPA 1999; Muller and Mendelsohn 2007). However, the integrated assessment model is used in a different way in this book. Rather than calculating the total damages due to total emissions, the model is used to calculate the marginal damages of emissions from individual sources for six of the major air pollutants

FIGURE I-2
INTEGRATED ASSESSMENT MODEL STRUCTURE

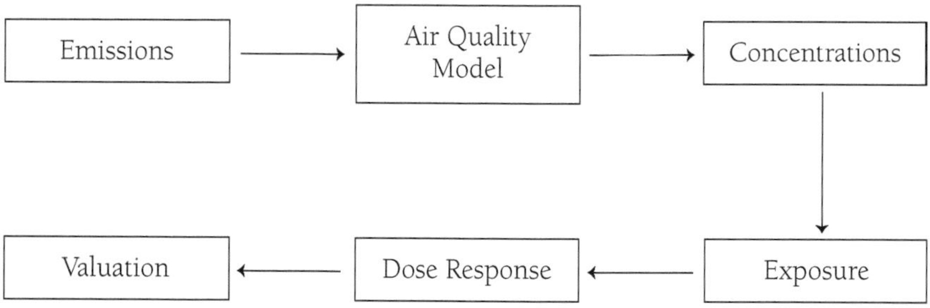

SOURCE: Authors' illustration.

measured by the USEPA.[1] Focusing on individual sources is essential when modeling these pollutants because marginal damages can vary significantly by location and by pollutant. For example, emissions in locations close to large metropolitan areas often cause large damages on a per-ton basis because such emissions affect many people. In contrast, emissions in remote locations generally produce much smaller damages per ton. Because efficient policy must recognize these differences, the model must reflect and quantify these differences if it is to be used to design efficient regulations.

This book is divided into ten chapters with an introduction and conclusion. In chapter 1, we review the economic theory of environmental regulation. The chapter considers abstract regulatory approaches from technology and performance standards to cap-and-trade programs and emission taxes. This chapter emphasizes that, although current versions of cap-and-trade programs and emission taxes are cost-effective, they do not reflect the marginal damage of emissions for specific sources. Efficient regulations require source-specific regulations that reflect local marginal damages. We show how both cap-and-trade programs and emission taxes can achieve economic efficiency. Cap-and-trade programs should have a matrix of fixed exchange rates that reflect the marginal damages in each location. Emission taxes must vary according to the marginal damage of emissions. The chapter stresses that efficient taxes and cap-and-trade programs prioritize abatement on the basis of damages and not tonnage.

After chapter 1, we move to part I, "The Integrated Assessment Model." This part, which includes chapters 2 through 5, explores various aspects of the model. Chapters 2 and 3 present the details. Chapter 2 describes the air quality model used in the integrated assessment model to estimate air pollution concentrations across the contiguous United States. The model translates emissions estimates across all sources and all counties in the contiguous United States, through physical transport and chemical transformation, into local air pollution concentrations in each county. This chapter presents two different approaches to developing air quality models: a process-based model and a simple reduced-form model. We show that the two models produce very similar predicted pollution surfaces. Because we

---

1. These include five of the criteria air pollutants (fine particulate matter, sulfur dioxide, nitrogen oxides, volatile organic compounds, coarse particulate matter), and ammonia.

require a model that permits policy evaluations that require many iterations, and because the models yield comparable results, we employ the simpler model throughout the remaining analyses in the book.

Chapter 3 introduces the remainder of the integrated assessment model that connects ambient air pollution concentrations to physical impacts and monetary damages. The chapter describes the calculation of exposures, physical impacts through the use of dose-response relationships, and valuation.

Chapters 4 and 5 present the raw results of the integrated assessment model. Chapter 4 describes the marginal damage of emissions across the United States. Past studies using integrated assessment models tended to calculate aggregate damages from large changes in emissions or from spatially aggregated sources. Our analysis focuses on marginal damages. The experimental design features the addition of a ton of emissions to baseline emissions at a specific source. The algorithm computes the change to aggregate baseline damages due to the additional ton. The change in aggregate damages caused by this added ton is the marginal damage. The estimated marginal damages are then presented for ten thousand sources in the United States and for six pollutants.

Chapter 5 describes the uncertainty associated with these marginal damage estimates. We focus on a case study of power plants and conduct a Monte Carlo analysis in order to generate empirical distributions for the marginal damages of SO_2 and fine particulate matter ($PM_{2.5}$). The marginal damages are quite variable, and the distributions are right-skewed. We also present results that show how the impacts of an emission are distributed downwind of that emission. If damages reflect lower realizations from the distribution, the impacts of an emission from a midwestern power plant are highly localized. However, with higher realizations from the distribution of damages, the impacts are spread throughout the Midwest, South, and East Coast.

Part II is titled "Policy Applications." This part, which includes chapters 6 and 7, explores two policy applications of the model. In chapter 6, we use the marginal damages to design efficient pollution control regulations for power plants in the United States. We consider the merits of both an efficient set of taxes and an efficient differentiated cap-and-trade program. The chapter illustrates how an efficient program would change emissions from over two thousand electric generating units in the United States. The analysis also discusses how the efficient regulations would be different from current cost-effective (uniform emission tax rates or undifferentiated trading) regulations. The analysis calculates the approximate potential gain in welfare due to moving from cost-effective to efficient regulations for this group of sources.

In chapter 7, we explain how consideration of marginal damages and marginal costs would allow regulators to prioritize emissions for either tighter or more relaxed regulation. Emissions whose marginal damages far exceed marginal abatement costs need stricter regulations to reduce emissions. Emissions whose marginal costs exceed marginal damages, however, are overregulated. Although it may seem obvious to focus on net marginal effects, current regulations are often more focused on tonnage than on net marginal effects. That is, in certain instances, very harmful emissions that involve little tonnage are given a low priority for abatement, while sources that emit large amounts of pollution but that cause very low damages are overregulated. The approach to reforming current policy presented in chapter 7 acknowledges that a wholesale change to efficient regulations is unlikely. However, the chapter argues that efficiency criteria can be used to conduct marginal reforms that stand to improve the efficiency of current policies.

Part III, "Measurement of Air Pollution Damages," which includes chapters 8 through 10, discusses various aspects of damage measurement and accounting. In chapter 8, we estimate the gross external damage (GED) of air emissions. GED is a measure of the total air pollution damage in the United States. GED relies on a methodology that is analogous to gross domestic product (GDP). GDP measures the value of total economic activity by multiplying the market price for goods and services times the quantity produced. GED computes the total "value" of air pollution damages by multiplying the marginal damage of each emission times the corresponding quantity of emissions. This is a first step to a system of environmental accounting for the United States. We examine what share of GED is caused by each pollutant and what share of total damages is due to damages to human health, agriculture, timber, visibility, materials, and recreation. We also compare the damages from each of the six local pollutants in this study and carbon dioxide (CO_2) emissions in the United States.

In chapter 9, we explore the components of GED by sector of the U.S. economy, including utilities, manufacturing, and agriculture. We compare the GED for every sector of the economy to the value added (VA) of that sector. This comparison provides a useful benchmark of the air pollution damage caused by each sector relative to the value of market production generated in that sector.

Chapter 10 measures the GED from air pollution produced by each industry in order to build more detailed environmental accounts. We report the GED produced by coal power plants, livestock operations, oil refineries, and many other polluting industries in the U.S. economy. Once again we compare the air pollution damage to the value of market production by industry. The analysis reveals several industries with very high damage to value-added ratios.

We conclude the book with a brief review of our fundamental results and their implications for policy. In general, regulators should place a higher priority on reducing urban, ground-level emissions because the marginal damage from such emissions is higher than for other sources. However, there is an important exception to this rule for nitrogen oxides where the atmospheric chemistry suggests that ground-level urban emissions are less harmful (and sometimes even beneficial). The observed variation in marginal damages means that environmental regulations must take into account marginal damages if they are to be allocatively efficient. For example, marginal damages can help regulators identify where to tighten and where to relax current regulations. Furthermore, designing efficient regulations needs to reflect the fact that the damage per ton varies considerably depending on where it is emitted. Therefore, the tax rates on emissions must vary across space depending on marginal damage. Cap-and-trade programs must employ trading ratios, or exchange rates, that reflect the differences in damages across space. We also point out that certain industries appear to be underregulated once damages from pollution are taken into account. Their GED exceeds their conventionally measured value added. Air pollution regulations of these industries are in urgent need of reform to mitigate the social costs associated with production.

Although there are many advantages to designing efficient regulatory programs, certain difficulties might arise in practice if new rules are implemented. How many different prices or exchange rates make sense? Will the system be too complicated? Will pollution migrate from one place to another, and is this acceptable? How often should the system be updated? How will firms adapt to the new regulations?

A great deal of work remains to be done to integrate information on costs and benefits into prospective improvements to air pollution regulation in the United States. The methods and analyses in this book prepare the way for the additional research necessary to make the leap to efficient regulations.

1

The Theory of Environmental Regulation

We begin with a brief review of environmental regulation—from the absence of regulation, to approaches that specify emission limits or certain abatement technologies, to market-based approaches including emission taxes and tradable permits. We show how these approaches represent a progression from a relatively crude beginning to a more sound, cost-effective approach. Presently, the United States has a mixture of ambient, performance, and technology standards as well as cost-effective market-based policies in place.

However, we believe that there is a superior policy alternative to present U.S. policy. After our review, we argue that an efficient policy is superior even to a cost-effective policy. We consider both an efficient emission tax and an efficient permit system and show that efficient programs promise a substantial reduction in *social* costs: the sum of environmental damages plus abatement costs. In later chapters, we will argue that it is now time to replace current U.S. pollution policy with an efficient policy.

Historical Approaches to Pollution Regulation in the United States

The United States and other countries have developed increasingly sophisticated approaches to environmental regulation over the past decades. We begin here by showing why some regulation is superior to completely unregulated markets and how each new policy approach has tended to represent an improvement over earlier approaches.

The Unregulated Market. Before the government imposed pollution regulations, firms tended to minimize expenditures aimed at reducing

11

emissions.[1] As profit maximizers, the firms looked at their various inputs (capital, labor, materials, and pollution) and chose the combination that led to the highest profits. More formally, they maximized profit (π) subject to a production function and market prices:

$$\max \pi = P_Q Q(K,L,M,X) - P_K K - P_L L - P_M M - P_X X \qquad (1.1)$$

where P_z is the price of good or input z, K is capital, L is land, M is materials, and X is emissions. The first-order condition for each input is:

$$\begin{aligned} P_Q \frac{\partial Q}{\partial K} &= P_K \\ P_Q \frac{\partial Q}{\partial L} &= P_L \\ P_Q \frac{\partial Q}{\partial M} &= P_M \\ P_Q \frac{\partial Q}{\partial X} &= P_X \end{aligned} \qquad (1.2)$$

There are market prices the firm must pay to use inputs K, L, and M. However, in the absence of regulation, the price of pollution was effectively zero. Seeking to minimize total costs, or equating the marginal cost of abatement to zero, the firm spends no resources to reduce emissions. Of course, the firm will not incur costs in order to emit more pollution, so there is a limit to its emissions even without regulation. However, these emissions will likely continue to grow as the production of output increases if no regulatory constraints exist.

Technology Standards. Against a backdrop of rapidly increasing emissions, regulators began to explore ways to restrict emissions. One of the most direct approaches was to mandate the adoption of specific pollution control technologies. These regulations were generally end-of-pipe technologies. Other forms of technology standards have been used in the United States. A prime example is the requirement for automobile manufacturers to install catalytic converters in vehicles in order to reduce emissions. In terms of (1.1), a technology standard would entail a specific combination of K, L, and M that would lead to a target level of X. Mandating specific technologies

---

1. We assume that there are no preexisting distortions such as income taxes (Goulder 2002).

is excessively costly because the production function of each firm and the input prices each faces are not the same. Mandating a specific technology may raise the cost of achieving any given level of emission control for a firm. That is, there may exist less expensive abatement strategies for certain firms than the technology specified by the government. This approach to regulating emissions does not permit or inspire firms to search for relatively inexpensive ways to reduce emissions. As a result, mandatory abatement technologies are rarely cost-effective.

Performance Standards. A slightly more cost-effective approach involves the use of performance standards; such a policy consists of mandates that firms limit their emissions to a certain amount. This approach tends to be less costly than technology standards because firms can identify *and* implement the least costly technology to reach the specified performance standard, given their specific labor and capital constraints. The ability of performance standards to incentivize firms to search for, identify, and implement what they determine to be the least-cost compliance choice suggests that this tack is generally more cost-effective (less expensive per unit emission reduction) than mandating technologies.

Performance standards require a slightly different regulatory apparatus than does a system based on technology standards. That is, with a mandated technology, regulators must focus enforcement on whether firms, either through end use or in the supply chain, are employing particular devices that yield emission reductions. In contrast, performance standards require that regulators monitor actual emissions, hence, performance. Because of the large number of individual sources for some regulated source types, such as vehicles, ensuring compliance with performance standards is impractical. Therefore, we tend to see technology standards for these source types. However, for large industrial installations such as power plants, emissions are discharged from a relatively small number of fixed point sources. For these sources it is feasible to design and implement performance standards. Correspondingly, this is where one observes such policies in practice.

More formally, we express each firm's abatement costs as a function of emissions (X) and output (Q). $C_i(X_i, Q_i)$ represents the combination of inputs that achieves each level of emissions at least cost for firm (i) In this case, we are envisioning emissions as an output that is linked to the level of production. The abatement cost function is:

$$C_i(X_i, Q_i)$$

(1.3)

where:

$$\frac{\partial C_i}{\partial X_i} \leq 0$$

$$\frac{\partial^2 C_i}{\partial X_i^2} \geq 0$$

By including the subscript (i), we are allowing the cost function and the marginal cost function of each firm to be different. When a regulator sets a specific rule that all firms can emit only a fixed level of emissions, the heterogeneity of cost functions across firms may cause the marginal cost of abatement to vary from polluter to polluter, as shown in (1.4)

$$\frac{\partial C_i(\overline{X})}{\partial X_i} \neq \frac{\partial C_j(\overline{X})}{\partial X_j}$$

(1.4)

As argued above, performance standards are often less costly than technology mandates, but they are rarely cost-effective. That is, performance standards do not minimize the total abatement cost of reaching a specified aggregate emission target. The inefficiency stems from the fixed, common limit on discharges across firms regulated under the standard; with uniform emission limits across all firms, if firms have heterogeneous abatement cost functions, then firms will not equate marginal costs in complying with a performance standard (Montgomery 1972). Some firms will be spending a lot, in a relative sense, to remove the last (marginal) ton of emission, whereas others will likely be spending relatively little. These rules lead to more wasteful abatement practices in the sense that they are excessively costly aggregate abatement programs. Provided an extant system of performance standards with firms that have heterogeneous abatement cost functions, society, through public policy, could lower the total costs spent on abatement by increasing emissions at sources facing relatively high abatement costs and by concurrently increasing abatement at sources facing relatively low abatement costs. Provided the effect on tonnage is offsetting, and the impact of each ton is the same, there is no change in environmental quality. The expensive abatement conducted by the high-cost firms is wasteful, because society could instead rely on less expensive abatement conducted by firms with lower abatement costs. The impetus for the policies discussed in the next section is to design mechanisms that allow firms to determine who executes more or less abatement subject to the overall limit on emissions, because firms will have a clearer sense of the relative abatement costs that they face.

Cost-effective Policy: Emission Taxes and Tradable Permits. To increase the cost-effectiveness of pollution policy, economists have advocated two broad market-based approaches to regulate pollution: emission taxes (Baumol and Oates 1988) and tradable permits (Dales 1968; Montgomery 1972; Tietenberg 1980). While European nations (including Denmark, Norway, and Sweden) have implemented uniform SO_2 taxes, the United States has used tradable permits to control SO_2 emissions from power plants and NO_x emissions from power plants and industrial point sources. These permit systems feature undifferentiated permits. That is, regulated firms trade allowances on a ton-for-ton basis. The goal of both policies is cost-effectiveness: achieving aggregate emission limits at a minimum total cost. The taxes minimize aggregate abatement costs at a prespecified price for emissions. The trading regimes minimize the aggregate abatement cost of a prespecified aggregate pollution target.

The uniform tax, t, is charged for each unit of emission regardless of where it is emitted. In the presence of such a policy, to maximize profit, firms minimize the sum of the abatement costs plus the tax payments:

$$\min x_i[C_i(X_i) + tX_i] \tag{1.5}$$

As many economists have pointed out, the solution to this problem is for each firm to equate its marginal abatement cost to the tax rate:

$$\frac{\partial C_i(X_i)}{\partial X_i} = t \tag{1.6}$$

Because all the firms face the same tax rate, this leads firms to equate their marginal costs to each other.

$$\frac{\partial C_i(X_i)}{\partial X_i} = \frac{\partial C_j(X_j)}{\partial X_j} \qquad (1.7)$$

The total abatement cost of achieving the level of aggregate emissions (the sum of emissions across all the firms) is a function of the tax rate. However, the condition in (1.7) indicates that the tax minimizes the total abatement costs associated with the corresponding emission level. Therefore the tax is cost-effective. There is no way to reallocate the emissions across polluters that will lead to a lower aggregate cost (Montgomery 1972).

An alternative approach is to use an undifferentiated permit system; this is an alternative known in policy circles as cap and trade. The regulator sets an aggregate cap on emissions (X_c) and allocates permits for this total across the regulated firms. The regulator's objective is to minimize the sum of abatement costs, subject to the constraint that the sum of the emissions of the (N) regulated firms is equal to the aggregate cap (X_c). The initial allocation of permits, denoted (X_i^o) for firm (i), is generally not designed to equate the marginal costs across firms. The initial allocation is based on historic emissions or some uniform rule. However, by making permits tradable, firms can adjust their emissions levels by exchanging permits that will lead to a cost-effective outcome.

When firms are faced with tradable permits and a permit price P, firms minimize their abatement costs, $C_i(X_i)$, plus the cost of buying permits from the $(N-1)$ other firms, $(\Sigma_j(PX_{bij})$, for $j = 1, \ldots, N-1)$, minus the revenue from selling permits (PX_{si}). If $-(\partial C_i(X_i^o)/(\partial Xi) < P$, firm (i) will sell permits. If $-(\partial C_i(X_i^o)/(\partial Xi) > P$, firm (i) will buy permits. A firm with sufficient initial permits can make a profit (negative costs) from selling permits. Provided that the aggregate emission constraint is binding, a firm's cost minimization objective is subject to a constraint for each firm (i) that emissions (X_i) must be equal to the initial allocation of permits (X_i^o) minus site (i) permits sold (X_{si}) plus permits purchased $\Sigma_j(X_{bij})$, for $j = 1, \ldots, N-1$:

$$\min x_i[C_i(X_i) + P(\sum_{j=1}^{N-1} X_{bij} - X_{si})]$$

$$\text{s.t. } X_i = X_i^0 - X_{si} + \sum_{j=1}^{N-1} X_{bij} \qquad (1.8)$$

The firm will choose to produce the level of emissions that equates its marginal cost of abatement to the market price for permits (see Muller and Mendelsohn 2009).

$$\frac{\partial C(X_i)}{\partial X_i} = P \tag{1.9}$$

Because the price of permits is the same for all firms, all the firms will equate their marginal costs with each other. The outcome is cost-effective, and it bears a close resemblance to the outcome in (1.7) associated with the uniform emission tax.

Efficient Policy: Spatially Explicit Taxes and Permit Trading

Although cost-effective market programs are an improvement over command-and-control policies, cost-effective policies are not always efficient. Trading ton for ton is efficient only if the marginal damage is the same for all polluters. Efficient policies minimize the sum of pollution damages plus abatement costs, in contrast to cost-effective policies, which focus only on minimizing abatement costs. In order to achieve efficiency, regulations must equate the marginal cost of abatement to the marginal damage of emissions for every source (Baumol and Oates 1988). Because the marginal damages of many air pollutants vary according to source location, policies governing these pollutants that equate marginal cost in every location are not efficient. Instead, efficiency requires that marginal damages be an integral part of regulatory design.

We use a theoretical model that includes damages as well as abatement costs in order to explore the efficiency of regulatory policies. We assume the regulator knows firm-specific marginal damages with certainty. The damages due to emissions from firm (i) are represented by the function $D_i(X_i)$. The damage from each emission by firm (i) reflects the sum of the damages to all of the victims exposed to that emission. We assume that $(\partial D_i(X_i)/\partial X_i) > 0$ and $(\partial^2 D_i(X_i)/\partial X_i^2) \geq 0$.

An efficient program minimizes the sum of abatement cost and damages across all firms (Baumol and Oates 1988):

$$\min_{Xi} \sum_{i=1}^{N} C_i(X_i) + \sum_{i=1}^{N} D_i(X_i) \tag{1.10}$$

The solution to this problem is:

$$\frac{\partial D_i}{\partial X_i} = -\frac{\partial C_i}{\partial X_i} \qquad (1.11)$$

Efficiency requires that the marginal abatement cost should equal the marginal damage for each polluting firm (i). If the marginal damages are not the same across firms, the marginal costs should not be the same, either. This is why, for pollutants with marginal damages that vary spatially, cost-effective programs, such as uniform taxes and undifferentiated permits, tend not to be efficient.

Although most researchers in the natural science community recognize that the damages from some pollution emissions often depend on where the emissions are released (e.g., Mauzerall et al. 2005), this is not captured by uniform taxes or cap-and-trade policies. Economists have wrestled with how to include location-specific damages into policy design. For example, allowance-trading regimes could be adjusted to reflect spatially variant damages. In particular, regions governed by a cap-and-trade program could be subdivided into districts, within which the marginal damages of emissions are homogenous. This approach would then allow ton-for-ton trading within each district because the marginal effects are common across sources *within* each district (Tietenberg 1980). The shortcoming of this approach is that it may lead to thin markets, with potentially few buyers and sellers of allowances in each market.

Another strategy establishes markets for ambient permits at each receptor point (Montgomery 1972; Baumol and Oates 1988). With this instrument, firms would have to buy ambient permits in each market affected by their emissions. This policy design has not been adopted because it is not practical; firms would have to participate in many different markets because every emission will affect environmental quality in many areas. It would likely be very costly for each firm to determine how its emissions impact local concentrations in each receptor location.

Another approach involves the use of a system of pollution offsets. This design requires each new or expanding source to buy offsets from existing sources if its emissions violate an ambient standard (Atkinson and Tietenberg 1982; Krupnick et al. 1983). The pollution offset approach suffers from the same general problem of complexity found in the ambient permit systems. Firms would have to know the impact of their emissions on local concentrations across potentially many receptor locations. Determining these effects would likely be prohibitively difficult and costly for firms.

In order to achieve efficiency (rather than just abatement cost-effectiveness), policies must be based on the marginal damage of each emission rather than just on abatement costs or tonnage. The literature in economics has long recognized that cost-effectiveness can be achieved with either taxes or tradable permits. The key to seeking efficiency is that the emission tax rates or the allowance prices must be tailored to the marginal damage of each regulated source. For example, emission taxes could be calibrated so that the marginal tax rate on emissions is equal to the marginal damage of emissions at each source location (Baumol and Oates 1988). Trading regimes could also be designed to reflect spatially variant damages. The regulator could establish trading ratios that reflect the ratio of the marginal damage of emissions between any pair of sources (Klaassen et al. 1994; Farrow et al. 2005). These fixed exchange rates determine the number of tons abated by one source that is required to offset the damage caused by an additional ton emitted by another source. This arrangement induces firms to trade in terms of the value of marginal damages instead of the quantity of emissions. Combining such trading ratios with an optimal cap on emissions can make cap-and-trade programs allocatively efficient.

A Firm's Response to Efficient Policy. A spatially explicit tax scheme would levy different tax rates on each regulated source location. The tax rate, established by the regulator, should be set equal to the marginal damages.

$$t_i = \frac{\partial D_i}{\partial X_i} \text{ for all } (i) \tag{1.12}$$

A firm faced with a differentiated emission tax (t_i) confronts a cost-minimization problem quite similar to equation (1.5) except that the tax rate is now location specific (t_i).

$$\min_{X_i} C_i(X_i) + t_i X_i \tag{1.13}$$

Differentiating the above expression with respect to X_i, setting equal to zero, and rearranging yields (1.14) indicates that the abatement cost minimizing outcome for firms is to abate until their marginal abatement cost is equated to the location-specific tax rate (t_i):

$$t_i = -\left(\frac{\partial C_i}{\partial X_i}\right)\nabla_i \qquad (1.14)$$

Given that the tax rate is equal to the marginal damage for each firm, this leads to the efficient outcome:

$$\frac{\partial D_i}{\partial X_i} = -\frac{\partial C_i}{\partial X_i} \text{ for all } (i) \qquad (1.15)$$

We now explore how a differentiated permit trading system works. The regulator chooses an initial distribution of permits across the (N) firms (where X_i^o denotes the allocation of permits to firm (i)) that leads to a target aggregate level of total damages (TD):

$$TD = \sum_{i=1}^{N} X_i^o \left(\frac{\partial D_i}{\partial X_i}\right) \qquad (1.16)$$

We assume that this target is binding on the polluters—that is, that it forces some aggregate abatement.

One objective that the regulator might pursue is to minimize the sum of abatement costs across all firms subject to TD:

$$\min_{Xi} \sum_{i=1}^{N} C_i(X_i) \qquad (1.17)$$

such that

$$TD = \sum_{i=1}^{N} X_i^o \left(\frac{\partial D_i}{\partial X_i}\right)$$

The Lagrangian expression corresponding to equation (1.17) is:

$$L = \sum_{i=1}^{N} C_i(X_i) - \rho\left(TD - \sum_{i=1}^{N} X_i^o \left(\frac{\partial D_i}{\partial X_i}\right)\right) \qquad (1.18)$$

where (ρ) is a Lagrange multiplier. The optimal solution to (1.18) is:

$$\rho\left(\frac{\partial D_i}{\partial X_i}\right) = -\frac{\partial C_i}{\partial X_i} \qquad (1.19)$$

Condition (1.19) suggests that marginal costs should be proportional to marginal damages. Intuitively, one implication of this condition is that society should spend more resources on abating emissions that cause more damage. Equation (1.19) implies that the ratio of marginal costs for any two firms (i) and (j) should be equal to the ratio of marginal damages:

$$\frac{\left(\frac{\partial D_i}{\partial X_i}\right)}{\left(\frac{\partial D_j}{\partial X_j}\right)} = \frac{\left(\frac{\partial C_i}{\partial X_i}\right)}{\left(\frac{\partial C_j}{\partial X_j}\right)} \quad \nabla_j \tag{1.20}$$

In an efficient cap-and-trade program, the regulator must establish the trading ratio (TR_{ij}) between any two polluting sources (i and j). Because firms are allowed to trade permits on a ton-for-ton basis, this ratio is equal to one in the undifferentiated permit system. However, the ratios should be different from one for any pair of sources with different marginal damages. The regulator must set TR_{ij} equal to the inverse ratio of marginal damages:

$$TR_{ij} = \frac{\Delta X_i}{\Delta X_j} = \frac{\frac{\partial D_j}{\partial X_j}}{\frac{\partial D_i}{\partial X_i}} \tag{1.21}$$

where ΔX_i equals the number of tons firm (i) can emit due to a concurrent reduction of ΔX_j tons of emission from firm (j). By setting the trading ratios in such a manner, the regulator is encouraging firms to trade in terms of the marginal damages of emissions instead of tonnage. As is the case in many markets for more conventional goods and services, trading reflects the relative value of the good being exchanged (emissions in this case) rather than the quantity of goods being exchanged.

Rearranging equation (1.21) displays a key property of the differentiated cap-and-trade program; trading between any two polluting sources (i) and (j) does not change total damages (Farrow et al. 2005):

$$\Delta X_i \left(\frac{\partial D_i}{\partial X_i}\right) - \Delta X_j \left(\frac{\partial D_j}{\partial X_j}\right) = 0 \tag{1.22}$$

Returning to equation (1.19), we see that for the level of total damages to be efficient, the optimal damage cap (TD^*) must equate marginal cost to marginal damage, a condition that implies $\rho = 1$. If the cap is set too high, implying too many emissions are produced, the firms together will not spend enough on abatement. If the cap is set too low, implying an overly strict cap, the firms together will spend too much on abatement.

We now show how firms will respond to the differentiated permit system. We assume that firms have cost minimization as their objective. Firm (i) begins with an initial allocation of permits (X_i^o) and a set of trading ratios calibrated and designated by the regulator. We assume that the initial allocation of permits is somewhat arbitrary, in that it is determined by some combination of historical production, equity, and political power. The set of TR_{ij} governs trades between firm (i) and all of the other $(N-1)$ sites (j). Firm (i) can abate, buy permits, or sell permits at the market price P_i. Firm (i) seeks to minimize its costs, subject to the constraint that its emissions (X_i) must be equal to the initial allocation of permits (X_i^o) minus site i permits sold (X_{si}) plus the sum of permits purchased from the other participating sites (j) weighted by its trading ratios $(\Sigma_j X_{bij} TR_{ij})$.

$$\min C_i(X_i) + (\sum_{j=1}^{N-1} P_j X_{bij} - P_i X_{si}) \tag{1.23}$$

$$\text{s.t. } X_i = X_i^0 - X_{si} + \sum_{j=1}^{N-1} X_{bij} TR_{ij}$$

The Lagrangian associated with this problem is:

$$L_i = C_i(X_i) - P_i X_{si} + \sum_{j=1}^{N-1} P_j X_{bij} - \phi_i \left(X_i - X_i^0 + X_{si} - \sum_{j=1}^{N-1} X_{bij} TR_{ij} \right) \tag{1.24}$$

where ϕ_i is a Lagrange multiplier. The solution for source (i) is:

$$\frac{\partial C_i}{\partial X_i} = P_i = P_j / TR_{ij} \tag{1.25}$$

(For the full derivation of this solution, see Muller and Mendelsohn 2009.) The firm (i) conducts abatement until its marginal abatement cost is equal to the price of selling its permits or buying a permit from any site j. If the marginal costs of abatement are less than the extant price for their permits, $-(\partial C_i(X_i^o)/\partial X_i) < P_i$, the firm will sell some permits because other firms will pay more for the permits than it costs firm i to abate. If marginal costs are less than the permit price *at zero pollution emissions*, $-(\partial C_i(0)/\partial X_i) \leq P_i$, the firm will not emit any pollution and will sell all of its initial permits. If the marginal costs of abatement are greater than the weighted price for other firms' permits, $-(\partial C_i(X_i^o)/\partial X_i) > P_j/TR_{ij}$, then the firm will want to buy some permits from firm j because it is cheaper for firm (i) to buy some permits than pay the marginal cost of abatement. Market forces will cause the weighted market prices to be equated $P_i = P_j/TR_{ij}$. Because the trading ratios are set so that $TR_{ij} = (\partial D_j/\partial X_j)/(\partial D_i/\partial X_i)$, this implies that $P_i/P_j = (\partial D_i/\partial X_i)/(\partial D_j/\partial X_j)$: the ratio of permit prices is equal to the ratio of marginal damages across firms. Given that the firms' response is to equate their marginal costs of abatement to the price of buying permits, $P_i/P_j = (-\partial C_i/\partial X_i)/(-\partial C_j/\partial X_j)$, the implication is that the firm ends up equating marginal costs to marginal damages: $(-\partial C_i/\partial X_i)/(-\partial C_j/\partial X_j) = (\partial D_i/\partial X_i)/(\partial D_j/\partial X_j)$. This is the efficiency condition in (1.20). This derivation shows that differentiated tradable permits are efficient.

This analysis assumes existing technology as fixed. However, both emission taxes and cap-and-trade regulations provide an incentive for firms to invest in research and development to find new technology that lowers their abatement costs. These incentives are slightly different for price and quantity instruments (Mendelsohn 1984). Efficient regulations will give firms in high-damage locations an even greater incentive to invest in technology that reduces emissions and abatement costs because of the relatively higher price that they face for permits.

Although clearly more complicated than the ton-for-ton current trading program, the proposed system of fixed exchange rates would be relatively simple for firms to use. The processes that link emissions to damages would be modeled by the regulator and embodied in the trading ratios. The trading ratios, made publicly known by the regulator, would govern subsequent trades between any two sources. Such exchanges would be weighted by the appropriate trading ratio. The firms would need to know only the current price for allowances, the trading ratios, and whether opportunities for arbitrage exist.

When faced with either spatially explicit tax rates or tradable exchange rates, each firm has an incentive to equate its marginal abatement cost to its own marginal damage, which leads to an efficient allocation of emissions. Both programs would encourage more abatement in places where emissions cause more damage. Of course, they would also allow more emissions in places where the damages are low. Although this is unlikely to lead to a great burden on individuals, care must be taken not to allow effects to become too inequitable. For example, the USEPA currently enforces air quality standards in every county in the contiguous United States. These ambient standards would act as a brake on a migration of emissions to any one particular source location.

PART I
The Integrated Assessment Model

2

Air Quality Modeling

Integrated assessment models (IAMs) link actions to consequences. An air pollution IAM links emissions to concentrations, to exposures, to physical effects, and ultimately to dollar damages. In this chapter we focus on the first of these links, between emissions and ambient concentrations. A key part of the IAM is the air quality model, which predicts the ambient concentrations that result from each emission. The air quality model has two major components. First, it captures the physical movement of gases and particles through space that is governed by prevailing weather and topography. The physical movement of gases is very important for estimating exposure, which is at the heart of many policy insights from IAMs. Second, it captures the atmospheric chemistry processes that transform emitted "primary" pollutants into "secondary" pollutants in the atmosphere.

There are two conceptual approaches to constructing an air quality model: process-based modeling and reduced-form modeling. The process-based model captures the complexities of environmental processes by including exhaustive representations of each mechanism in the atmosphere. The process-based models are considered to be the state-of-the-science approach because they most closely resemble the physical and chemical processes that link emissions to concentrations. The models are capable of linking emissions to concentrations at very fine spatial and temporal scales. Despite these advantages, there are downsides to these models. The models are complex and expensive to build and run. Their high cost limits the number of times researchers can run these models, which may be a critical constraint for applications in which many iterations are necessary. Thus, one cannot use such a model to estimate the impact of emissions from many individual sources, because it would be prohibitively costly. Furthermore, the complexity of the process-based models makes it difficult to isolate the influence of particular parameters in such a model on the results. Without the ability to conduct many repetitions, systematically testing the sensitivity to parameters in the model is often not possible. It may also be difficult to determine whether the model is operating properly, especially when it is being used in a policy context that deviates from the historical record.

The reduced-form modeling approach depicts the environment with a simple representation that mimics the overall behavior of the entire system. Reduced-form models do not include all the complex relationships of the process-based models. Their advantages are that they are fast, inexpensive, and easy to interpret. The most critical drawback of reduced-form models is that they may omit or misrepresent a key element in the environmental process. This may lead to biased results. As a result, it is important to use the process models to inform or calibrate reduced-form models. A second shortcoming of reduced-form models is that they may not predict some useful outcomes such as daily or hourly concentrations.

The Air Pollution Emission Experiments and Policy (APEEP) analysis model relies on a reduced-form model of air quality. The reduced-form air quality model is a variant of a Gaussian plume model (Turner 1994). We rely on this relatively simple Gaussian plume model because we need to be able to conduct multiple runs of the model in order to conduct policy analyses. In contrast to APEEP, the Air Pollution Impact Model (APIM) relies on a process-based model of air quality. The state-of-the-art process-based model in APIM is the Community Multiscale Air Quality (CMAQ) model (Byun and Schere 2006). We explain the differences between these two models and compare their predicted outputs in this chapter.

Both air quality models use estimates of emissions as inputs. In this analysis, we follow the consequences of six emitted pollutants: SO_2, VOCs, NO_x, $PM_{2.5}$, coarse particulate matter (PM_{10}), and ammonia (NH_3). The first five pollutants are regulated as "criteria pollutants" under the Clean Air Act because of their documented impact on human health. Ammonia, although not officially a criteria pollutant, influences concentrations of $PM_{2.5}$ and PM_{10}, both of which affect health, so we include it in the analysis. Although lead was originally a criteria pollutant, it has been successfully reduced through regulation to the point where it is no longer an important air pollutant in the United States.

For each of the six pollutants, emissions for each pollution source are estimated by the USEPA in its National Emissions Inventory (USEPA 2006).

In APEEP we track emissions from nearly ten thousand individual and grouped sources that fit into one of the following categories: mobile and area sources with emissions at ground level, point sources with an effective height of emissions of less than 250 meters, point sources with an effective height of emissions between 250 and 500 meters, and tall point sources (effective height greater than 500 meters). The 656 tall point sources tend to be relatively large emitters. They are modeled at the plant level in the model with exact latitude and longitude coordinates. The remaining sources are aggregated to the county level. The inventory measures the emissions of 3,110 counties across the contiguous United States for three emission heights (9,330 emission sources) plus 656 point sources, for a total of 9,986 unique sources of emissions.

Gaussian Plume Model

With the use of the emission inputs and weather data, including seasonal temperature, pressure, humidity and wind patterns, and simple functional representations of atmospheric chemistry, the Gaussian plume model predicts seasonal and annual average county concentrations of SO_2, NO_x, VOCs, $PM_{2.5}$, PM_{10}, and tropospheric ozone (O_3) for every county in the lower forty-eight states.[1] The air quality model uses a source-receptor matrix framework. A source-receptor matrix calculates the marginal contribution of emissions from each source to each receptor county.[2]

For both winter and summer, the model contains source-receptor matrices that model how emissions of NO_x and SO_2 disseminate across the landscape. The matrix also predicts the annual formation of particulates for the following pollutants: $NO_x \rightarrow PM_{2.5}$, $SO_2 \rightarrow PM_{2.5}$, $NH_3 \rightarrow NH_4$, and $VOCs \rightarrow PM_{2.5}$. Finally, there is a matrix that governs the relationship between NO_x emissions, VOC emissions, and O_3 concentrations in the summer season.

---

1. All computations that rely on meteorological data employ observations from the National Oceanic and Atmospheric Administration's Integrated Surface Hourly data sets for 1995–99.

2. The emission data provided by USEPA represent annual emissions in tons/year. These are converted to g/s, and the concentrations are predicted in g/m^3. These estimates are then converted to micrograms per cubic meter ($\mu g/m^3$), parts per billion by volume (ppbv), and parts per million by volume (ppmv) as needed.

The source-receptor matrices are derived from a variant of the Gaussian plume model (Turner 1994). Ambient concentrations, $C_{r,p}$ of a pollutant (p) at receptor county (r), are estimated using the following formula:

$$C_{r,p} = \sum_{s=1}^{S} \left[\left(\frac{E_s \theta_{sd} f_w f_d f_c}{\pi \mu_{sd} \sigma_{yd} \sigma_{zd}} \right) e^{\left(-\frac{H_{sd}^2}{2\sigma_z^2} \right)} \right] \tag{2.1}$$

where E_s is the emission from source s, $\theta_{s,d}$ denotes the probability that the wind blows from the direction, d, of the source county toward the receptor county, and H is the effective height of emissions. The effective height takes into account both the height of the smokestack and the lift in the emission from heat in the plume (Briggs 1969, 1971, 1975; Seinfeld and Pandis 1998; Turner 1994). Other key dispersion variables that depend on local weather include the wind speed, μ, the horizontal dispersion parameter, σ_y, and the vertical dispersion parameter, σ_z (Pasquill 1961). Both the horizontal dispersion parameter and the vertical dispersion parameter are increasing functions of distance between the source and the receptor; the greater the distance, the more dispersed the plume becomes. The Gaussian model also includes terms for wet and dry deposition (f_w and f_d) that remove pollution from the air. The model also captures the chemical transformation of pollution from one type to another, f_c.

Tropospheric ozone (O_3) formation is captured in a separate model. O_3 is a secondary pollutant formed by emissions of carbon monoxide (CO), NO_x and VOCs (Seinfeld and Pandis 1998). Ambient concentrations of tropospheric O_3 are predicted using an empirical model estimated using CO, VOCs, NO_x, and O_3 observations from the U.S. Environmental Protection Agency's AIRS (Aerometric Information Retrieval System: USEPA 2012) network as well as measurements of land use, temperature, time of day, and geographical factors. The specified model is:

$$\log O_3 = B_0 + B_1 t + B_2 t^2 + B_3 NO_x + B_4 NO_x^2 + B_5 VOC + B_6 VOC^2 + B_7 CO + B_8 CO^2 + B_9 F + B_{10} T + B_{11} G + \varepsilon \tag{2.2}$$

where hour of day, t, carbon monoxide, CO, percentage land area covered by four forest regimes and agricultural land use, F, temperature, T, and geography, G (latitude, longitude, altitude, metropolitan binary variable, and a California binary variable) all play a role. California is controlled for with a binary variable because of the unique conditions related to ozone formation in the state.

The model parameters, B, have been estimated using an ordinary least squares regression. The inclusion of both the linear and quadratic terms for NO_x, CO, and VOCs approximate the nonlinear effect of these gases on O_3 levels (Seinfeld and Pandis 1998). Specifically, the quadratic form captures the "titration effect" in areas where the background concentration of NO_x is high; in this situation, additional emissions of NO_x may cause O_3 concentrations to fall. This well-known relationship is critically important to capture in certain urban areas (Tong et al. 2006). The APEEP model uses equation 2.2 to predict the O_3 concentration in each county, given the predicted concentration of both the NO_x and VOCs concentrations in that county.

The formation of secondary particulates is captured by the atmospheric transformation rate constants, f_c, in equation (2.1). For the transformation of SO_2 and NO_x into particulates, APEEP uses constants derived from the Climatological Regional Dispersion Model (CRDM) (USEPA 2004). APEEP computes the ammonium-sulfate-nitrate equilibrium that determines the amount of ambient ammonium sulfate $(NH_4)_2SO_4$ and ammonium nitrate (NH_4NO_3) at each receptor county. The equilibrium computations reflect several fundamental aspects of this system. First, ambient ammonium (NH_4) reacts preferentially with sulfate (H_2SO_4). Second, ammonium nitrate is able to form only if there is excess NH_4 after reacting with sulfate. Finally, particulate nitrate formation is a decreasing function of temperature—so the ambient temperature at each receptor location is incorporated into the equilibrium calculations. In order to translate VOC emissions into secondary organic particulates, APEEP employs the fractional aerosol yield coefficients estimated by Grosjean and Seinfeld (1989). These coefficients represent the yield of particulates corresponding to emissions of gaseous VOCs.

Community Multiscale Air Quality Model

The CMAQ model is a process-based model of the atmosphere with advanced atmospheric chemistry modules (Byun and Schere 2006). CMAQ divides the atmosphere into grid cells along a horizontal plane and vertical plane. CMAQ then predicts air movements from one grid cell to another across both the vertical and the horizontal dimensions. Physical movements of parcels of air are based on observed hourly weather data. The size of each box (the resolution of the model) is determined by the researcher. More detailed boxes provide more geographic resolution but increasingly more expensive runs. CMAQ can predict concentrations based on either long-run average weather patterns (estimating "average" concentrations), and it can also model short-run episodic events. In contrast, the Gaussian plume model is designed strictly to model long-run average concentrations. CMAQ also has a very complex atmospheric chemistry module that captures each chemical transformation in the atmosphere (Byun and Schere 2006).

Comparing CMAQ and APEEP

We evaluate each air quality model by testing how well it predicts observed ambient concentrations. Starting with the National Emissions Inventory (USEPA 2006), one can test how well the predicted concentrations from each model match what is observed in the USEPA's AIRS monitor network (USEPA 2012). We compare the average ambient concentrations in each county predicted by each model to the averages from the monitor readings for each pollutant in each county with a monitoring station for the year 2002. For most pollutants, we focus on annual average readings. However, for O_3 we use hourly measurements averaged over the summer to determine whether we are capturing the fluctuations within a day correctly. One problem with using the AIRS data set is that it is not a random set of measurements across space. The monitors are frequently placed close to local sources of pollution, that is, in locations that exceed the ambient air standards. By averaging measurements across a county, we aim to reduce some of the bias associated with this placement. However, this does not completely eliminate the problem.

We follow the model evaluation literature and employ four error statistics: the mean error, the mean bias, the normalized mean error, and the normalized mean bias (Tong and Mauzerall 2006; USEPA 2005). Each of the following four statistics is computed for each pollutant. The mean error, ME, is the average of the difference in absolute values between predicted and observed observations:

$$ME = \frac{1}{N}\sum_{r=1}^{N}|A_r - C_r| \qquad (2.3)$$

where C_r is the arithmetic mean of the observed pollution in county (r), and A_r is the predicted concentration by the model. The mean bias, MB, is the average of the difference between observed and predicted values:

$$MB = \frac{1}{N} \sum_{r=1}^{N} (A_r - C_r) \qquad (2.4)$$

The normalized mean error, NME, is the proportional mean error:

$$NME = \frac{1}{N} \frac{\sum_{r=1}^{N} |A_r - C_r|}{\sum_{r=1}^{N} C_r} \qquad (2.5)$$

The normalized mean bias, NMB, is the proportional mean bias:

$$NMB = \frac{1}{N} \frac{\sum_{r=1}^{N} (A_r - C_r)}{\sum_{r=1}^{N} C_r} \qquad (2.6)$$

Finally, for each pollutant we compute the Pearson correlation coefficient (ρ). This procedure is helpful in determining if the spatial pattern of the predicted surfaces matches the distribution observed by the monitors.

$$\rho_{AC} = \frac{\sum_{r=1}^{N} (A_r - \bar{A})(C_r - \bar{C})}{\sigma_A \sigma_C} \qquad (2.7)$$

where $\bar{A}$ is the arithmetic mean of the predicted pollution, $\bar{C}$ is the arithmetic mean of the observed pollution, σ_A is the standard deviation of the predicted values, and σ_C is the standard deviation of the observed values.

We compare the results of these measurements for APEEP and CMAQ. Except for O_3, predictions from the CMAQ model have been averaged to reflect seasonal county arithmetic means. For O_3, predictions from the CMAQ model are averaged across the days in the simulation for each hour leading to twenty-four hourly readings. This matches the hourly output from APEEP.

Table 2-1 reports the performance of APEEP against available observations from the AIRS data set. The O_3 results are reasonably good. APEEP predicts O_3 levels that are slightly higher than the observed levels. However, the results compare well to the observed data across space. Comparable

TABLE 2-1

COMPARING **APEEP**-PREDICTED CONCENTRATIONS
TO OBSERVED CONCENTRATIONS

Species	Season	ME	MB	NME (%)	NMB (%)	ρ	N
O_3 (ppbv)	Summer	7.2	0.57	29	12	0.74	15,645
$PM_{2.5}$ (μg/m³)	Annual	4.4	−2.6	35	−20	0.33	181
SO_2 (ppbv)	Summer	1.5	−0.25	78	34	0.59	333
SO_2 (ppbv)	Winter	2.3	0.02	115	71	0.46	343
NO_x (ppbv)	Summer	9.5	−6.9	64	−22	0.41	166
NO_x (ppbv)	Winter	16.6	−3.7	79	27	0.39	170

SOURCE: Monitor Data, USEPA 2012.

results in the literature for CMAQ evaluations suggest APEEP's predictions are equally accurate with respect to the AIRS data (Tong and Mauzerall 2006). Russell and Dennis (2000) suggest that a NME of between 30 to 35 percent and an NMB of between ±5 to 15 percent is acceptable for O_3. The APEEP results for $PM_{2.5}$ are also quite good. The model slightly underestimates the amount of $PM_{2.5}$ observed in the atmosphere, with an NMB of −20 percent. The results compare well to a recent evaluation using a different observational data set and CMAQ. That study produced an ME of 5.5 (μg)/(m³), an MB of −2.1(μg)/(m³), an NME of 43 percent, and an NMB of −16 percent (USEPA 2005).

The SO_2 predictions by APEEP have very little error or bias. The results were quite similar to results using CMAQ that produced an ME of 1.36 (ppbv) and an MB of 0.82 (ppbv) for summer, and an ME of 2.3 (ppbv) and an MB of 0.02 (ppbv) for winter (USEPA 2005). The NME and NMB for APEEP were higher than the corresponding values for CMAQ in the USEPA study, but this may be because the USEPA study relied on the Clean Air Status and Trends Network (CASTNET) data rather than AIRS data. That is, the two studies did not use the same observations of pollution concentrations to make their comparisons. The NO_x results were not as good as the SO_2 results. APEEP underestimates NO_x levels and has a relatively large normalized error in both summer and winter.

The previous discussion compares the results from APEEP with the reported results in the literature using CMAQ, the state-of-the-art model.

Pollutant	Season	ME	MB	NME (%)	NMB (%)	ρ	N
NO_x (ppbv)	Summer	1.1	0.21	42	14	0.86	3,110
SO_2 (ppbv)	Summer	0.5	0.06	47	19	0.78	3,110
O_3 (24hr.) (ppbv)	Summer	10.0	0.01	21	0.3	0.69	74,640
O_3 (8hr.) (ppbv)	Summer	9.0	−8.6	16	−16	0.77	24,880
$PM_{2.5}$ ($\mu g/m^3$)	Annual	2.4	2.0	26	−19	0.85	3,110
PM_{10} ($\mu g/m^3$)	Annual	4.2	3.8	50	47	0.74	3,110

Although such comparisons are helpful, they are not a perfect test of the two models because they are not being compared across the same observations. The literature that tests CMAQ's performance relies on a more restrictive set of ambient air measurements from a limited set of places. In order to make a more direct comparison of the two models, we test how well APEEP can predict CMAQ outcomes for the same year and conditions.

In table 2-2, we use predicted concentrations from CMAQ as the basis for comparison in computing the four error statistics (ME, MB, NME, and NMB). We generate county-level predictions for 2002 from average emissions using the CMAQ model (we thank Daniel Tong for these predictions). We then test whether APEEP can generate the same predictions for concentrations in each county, given the same emission.

For $PM_{2.5}$ and O_3, APEEP's predicted levels are in good agreement with CMAQ's predictions. The bias is small, and the spatial correlations are high. The agreement is especially good for the eight-hour measures of O_3, implying that APEEP does a good job of capturing hourly changes in O_3. There are slightly larger but acceptable biases associated with NO_x and SO_2. The bias associated with the predictions of PM_{10}, however, are quite large. APEEP predicts substantially more PM_{10} than CMAQ. Overall, though, there is good agreement between the predictions of the two air quality models, especially for $PM_{2.5}$ and O_3.

In order to get a clearer picture of how closely the APEEP and CMAQ results are to one another, we have mapped $PM_{2.5}$ concentrations from both

FIGURE 2-1

APEEP PM$_{2.5}$ AMBIENT CONCENTRATIONS, ANNUAL MEAN, 2002 (µg/m³)

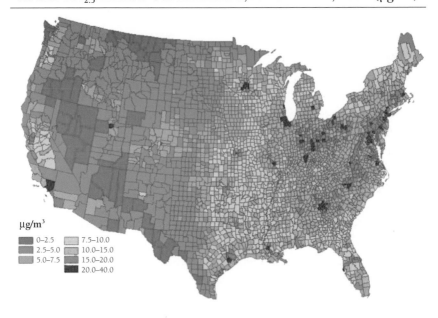

µg/m³

■ 0–2.5	▨ 7.5–10.0
■ 2.5–5.0	▨ 10.0–15.0
■ 5.0–7.5	▨ 15.0–20.0
	■ 20.0–40.0

models in figure 2-1 and figure 2-2. Figure 2-1 from APEEP reveals that PM$_{2.5}$ is high in most metropolitan areas and generally higher east of the Mississippi River. Figure 2-2 from CMAQ reveals the higher concentrations in large metropolitan areas and the same regional patterns as the APEEP map. However, APEEP seems to generate sharper distinctions across space than CMAQ. Because this is a direct comparison of two predictions, it is not a test of which model is correct. However, the fact that they both agree about general patterns provides confidence in the air quality modeling presented throughout our study.

Figures 2-3 and 2-4 compare the predictions of eight-hour O$_3$ concentrations across counties using the APEEP and CMAQ models respectively. Both models predict high ozone levels east of the Mississippi River and downwind of major metropolitan areas such as Atlanta, Detroit, and the northeast corridor between Washington, DC, and Boston. The values are slightly higher for APEEP in key metropolitan areas, but the differences in the spatial patterns between the two maps are small.

FIGURE 2-2

CMAQ PM$_{2.5}$ Ambient Concentrations, Annual Mean, 2002 (μg/m^3)

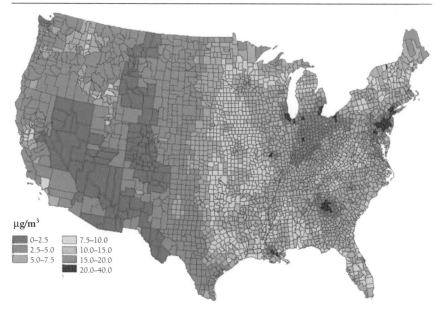

μg/m^3

- 0–2.5
- 2.5–5.0
- 5.0–7.5
- 7.5–10.0
- 10.0–15.0
- 15.0–20.0
- 20.0–40.0

FIGURE 2-3

APEEP O$_3$ Ambient Concentrations, Annual Mean, 2002 (ppbv)

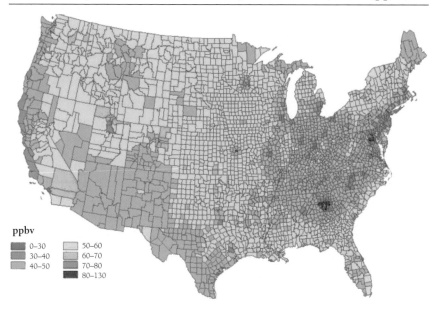

ppbv

- 0–30
- 30–40
- 40–50
- 50–60
- 60–70
- 70–80
- 80–130

FIGURE 2-4
CMAQ O₃ AMBIENT CONCENTRATIONS, ANNUAL MEAN, 2002 (ppbv)

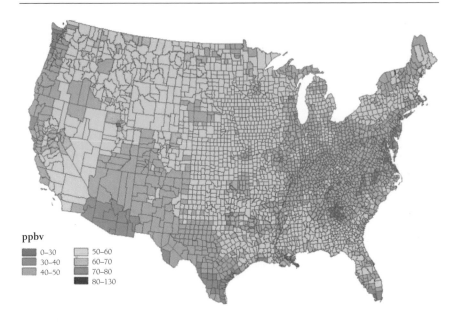

ppbv

■ 0–30	□ 50–60
■ 30–40	▨ 60–70
▨ 40–50	■ 70–80
	■ 80–130

These experiments show that APEEP is comparable to CMAQ in predicting average PM$_{2.5}$ and O$_3$ concentrations. The results indicate that the performance of APEEP is quite satisfactory, even though it uses a reduced-form approach to modeling a series of complex environmental processes. It is especially important that it models PM$_{2.5}$ and O$_3$ concentrations carefully, as these are the two most harmful pollutants that we examine. The performance of the air quality model in APEEP compares favorably with CMAQ. The strong agreement of these two air quality models is important because of the key role that air quality modeling plays within the larger IAM structure. Furthermore, the consistency of the air quality results in these models adds confidence to the central policy result of this book that marginal damages vary across space.

3

Modeling Air Pollution Impacts

As described in the introduction, an air pollution integrated assessment model links emissions to concentrations, to exposures, to physical effects, and, ultimately, to monetary damages. Having considered the link between emissions and ambient concentrations in the last chapter, we now consider how APEEP and APIM track exposures, calculate physical effects, and then value these physical effects in monetary terms. These last three steps are the same in both the APEEP and APIM models. The two models simply use different air quality models. APEEP relies on the Gaussian plume model, and APIM relies on CMAQ.

Exposures are calculated by multiplying the estimated county-level pollution concentrations of each pollutant times the county-level inventories of people, crops, trees, man-made materials, visibility resources, and sensitive ecosystems. Exposures are translated into physical effects using peer-reviewed concentration-response functions. These functions are drawn from published studies in each relevant discipline; for instance, epidemiological studies describe the relationship between human exposures to pollution and mortality rates, and agricultural studies link crop exposures to yields. These physical effects are valued in monetary terms using the findings from economic studies that report the marginal value of these various physical effects. Taken together, these three steps link concentrations of pollution to dollar damages.

Exposures

Because the consequences of policy are related to the number of sensitive receptors involved, APEEP calculates population-weighted exposures (PE) by multiplying sensitive populations in each receptor location by the concentration of pollution in that location.

$$PE_{pr} = P_r \left(A_{pr} \right) \tag{3.1}$$

where: PE_{pr} = population-weighted exposures to pollutant (p) in receptor county (r)

P_r = population in receptor county (r)

A_{pr} = predicted ambient concentration of pollutant (p) in receptor county (r)

It is important to note that the term "population" above refers to the inventory of sensitive receptors in a certain location. These inventories are defined generally to include people, crops, commercial timber, man-made materials, visibility resources, and forest resources used for recreation.

Exposures are modeled for each of these six distinct receptor types. The correct measurement of pollution exposures must correspond to the measure used in the dose-response studies. Most dose-response studies rely on the concentration of outdoor air pollution to measure pollution. In order to match the dose-response studies with the output from air quality models, APEEP models the predicted annual average concentrations of ambient air pollution in each receptor county.[1] The following discussion addresses how APEEP organizes a variety of data into populations of sensitive receptors and how the model computes exposures of people, crops, trees, man-made materials, visibility, and recreation resources.

Human Health. APEEP calculates human exposures to each pollutant separately for each of the nineteen age groups reported by the U.S. Census Bureau (2000). This permits an analysis of the air pollution exposures for people of different ages. Such detailed exposure analysis is particularly useful because the epidemiological literature indicates that pollution increases mortality risks in proportion to the baseline mortality rate of each age group of the population.[2] Because mortality rates increase dramatically with age, the elderly are more vulnerable to pollution exposures than younger

---

1. For O_3, APEEP models seasonal average concentrations.

2. The version of APEEP used herein contains an important update relative to the version of APEEP that has been used in prior applications (Muller and Mendelsohn 2007, 2009). In particular, the all-cause mortality rate data used here contain greater detail among the age groups of the population consisting of persons over sixty-five years of age. In prior applications, APEEP contained mortality rate data that consisted of average mortality rates across all persons over sixty-five.

populations. Differentiating the human population by age is therefore critical. Local exposures are calculated for each age group in each county. Different health outcomes can then be predicted for each age group.

Agriculture. APEEP models the effect that exposures to ozone (O_3) have on commercial crop yields. Exposures are calculated by multiplying reported county crop yields times the seasonal mean O_3 concentration. APEEP includes inventories of county-level yields for alfalfa, lettuce, tobacco, corn, cotton, peanuts, dry edible beans, grain sorghum, soybeans, spring wheat, and winter wheat from the Census of Agriculture (USDA 2002). The relationship between yields and pollution exposures depends on seasonal mean O_3 concentrations (Lesser et al. 1990).

Commercial Timber. APEEP focuses on the effect that exposures to O_3 have on commercial timber yields. The timber module measures exposures to O_3 concentrations separately for coniferous and broadleaf species groups (Hogsett et al. 1997; Pye 1988; Reich 1987). The model contains an inventory of the total growth of each species group in each county. The data are provided by the Forest Inventory and Analysis Database (USDA 2008). These data sets provide mortality (M), removals (R), and net growth (NG), from which the growth (G) by species group, by county, is derived. All measurements are expressed in cubic board feet.

$$G_{fr} = NG_{fr} + R_{fr} + M_{fr} \tag{3.2}$$

where: f = forest species group (hardwood, softwood)
r = receptor county

Exposures are computed by multiplying the growth (G_{fr}) times the seasonal mean O_3 level, by county and tree type.

Man-made Materials. Calculating exposures of man-made materials to air pollution requires the development of an inventory that characterizes the quantity of such materials in each county in the lower forty-eight states (Freeman 1982). APEEP calculates exposures of carbonate stone, galvanized steel, carbon steel, and painted wood surfaces to county seasonal average concentrations of SO_2. The model relies on county-level data collected by the Residential Energy Consumption Survey (U.S. Department of Energy 1992) and the Housing and Population Survey (U.S. Census Bureau 2000). The model computes the exposed surface area of each building in each receptor county. This depends on estimates of the number of buildings (including single-family homes, multifamily homes, and business establishments), the average structure size for each building type, and the probability of each material being used in each county.

Characteristics of commercial structures are gathered by the Commercial Energy Building Survey (U.S. Department of Energy 1993). The survey provides structure size in terms of floor space (ft²). Thus, with a simplifying assumption regarding the shape of the structure (we assume that each residential structure is cubic with two stories of living space), the conversion from floor space to wall space is straightforward. That is, the total area of living space is equivalent to twice the area of one story. Thus, given our cubic shape assumption, the area of the four walls is equivalent to four times the area of one story, or two times the total living area.

The calculations take the following form.

$$SA_{rm} = (N_{rt})(S_{rt})(P_{rm})\tag{3.3}$$

where: SA_{rm} = exposed surface area of building material (m) in receptor county (r)
N_{rt} = number of structures type (t) in county (r)
S_{rt} = area of exterior wall space per structure in county (r)
P_{rm} = probability material (m) used on exterior wall space in county (r)

For infrastructural materials (galvanized and painted carbon steel), the inventory relies on methods developed in the National Acid Precipitation Assessment Program (NAPAP), in particular the NAPAP surface-area estimates for galvanized and carbon steel (focusing on bridges, transmission towers, railroads, and guard rails) for the state of New York (U.S. National Acid Precipitation Assessment Program 1991a, 1991b). The ratios of exposed surface area to land area are then extrapolated to other geographic areas. Exposures are computed as the product of the estimated seasonal mean SO_2 concentrations and the estimated surface area of each material in each county.

Visibility. APEEP measures visibility using visual range (expressed in miles). The empirical studies that examine the economic significance of visibility calculate the willingness to pay for small changes in visibility at the household level (Chestnut and Rowe 1990, Chestnut and Dennis 1997). Thus, the relevant population for quantifying exposures is the number of households on the county level. Exposures are estimated by multiplying the number of households times the baseline visual range times the estimated seasonal mean PM_{10} concentration. The visual-range data are provided by the National Oceanic and Atmospheric Administration (NOAA)'s Integrated Surface Hourly weather databases (U.S. National Oceanic and Atmospheric Administration 2000).

Recreation. APEEP focuses on the incremental effects of air pollution exposures on recreation usage in forest ecosystems (U.S. National Acid Precipitation Assessment Program 1991b). APEEP calculates exposures as the acres of forested land in each county multiplied by the number of recreation visitor days (RVD) times the estimated ambient concentrations of O_3, NO_x, and SO_2. Recreation visitor day data are provided by several federal agencies, including the U.S. Department of the Interior and the U.S. Department of Agriculture, and by state governments (which manage recreation usage on state-owned lands) (U.S. National Acid Precipitation Assessment Program 1991b).

Dose Response

APEEP employs dose-response functions (also frequently called concentration-response functions and exposure-response functions) to translate ambient concentrations and exposures into various physical effects: hospital admissions, premature deaths, decreased agricultural and forestry yields, enhanced depreciation of man-made materials, reduced visibility, and declining recreation use. (See tables 3-1 through 3-4 for the list of dose-response functions used in this analysis.) APEEP relies on peer-reviewed studies to provide statistically estimated dose-response functions for the following fields: human health, agriculture, and man-made materials. Because peer-reviewed dose-response functions pertaining to timber, visibility, and changes in recreation use were not available at the time

TABLE 3-1

EPIDEMIOLOGY STUDIES EMPLOYED IN **APEEP**

Health Event	Pollutant	Study Author
Chronic Exposure Mortality	$PM_{2.5}$	Pope et al. (2002)
Chronic Exposure Mortality	$PM_{2.5}$	Laden et al. (2006)
Acute Exposure Mortality	$PM_{2.5}$	Klemm and Mason (2003)
Chronic Bronchitis	PM_{10}	Abbey et al. (1993)
Chronic Asthma	O_3	McDonnell et al. (1999)
Acute Exposure Mortality	O_3	Bell et al. (2004)
Respiratory Admissions	O_3	Schwartz and Morris (1995)
Emergency Room Visits—Asthma	O_3	Steib et al. (1996)
Chronic Obstructive Pulmonary Disease Admissions	NO_2	Moolgavkar (2000)
Ischemic Heart Disease Admissions	NO_2	Burnett et al. (1999)
Asthma Admissions	SO_2	Sheppard et al. (1999)
Cardiac Admissions	SO_2	Burnett et al. (1999)

APEEP was developed, the model uses data reported in peer-reviewed studies in these fields to estimate dose-response functional relationships, which are then employed directly in APEEP.

Human Health. APEEP relies on peer-reviewed studies in the epidemiological literature to model dose-response relationships between human health and exposures to air pollution. The default adult mortality dose-response function for exposures to $PM_{2.5}$ in APEEP is that reported in Pope et al. (2002). APEEP also uses the dose-response function reported in Laden et al. (2006) as an alternative to that reported in Pope et al. (2002). Findings from Bell et al. (2004) are used to capture the mortality effects of acute exposures to O_3. The impact of each air pollutant on the incidence rates of a variety of illnesses are modeled using the studies cited in table 3-1. Note that as new studies are published, the APEEP framework can easily be updated to employ new results.

The statistical models used to estimate dose-response functions are typically log-linear models.

$$log(H/Pop) = \alpha + \gamma X + \beta C + \varepsilon \tag{3.4}$$

TABLE 3-2
DOSE-RESPONSE FUNCTION PARAMETERS FOR O_3 AND AGRICULTURAL CROPS

Crop	Pollutant	γ	σ
Corn	O_3	2.83	0.124
Cotton	O_3	2.06	0.111
Peanut	O_3	2.27	0.109
Spring Wheat	O_3	2.56	0.136
Grain Sorghum	O_3	2.07	0.314
Alfalfa	O_3	1.78	0.179
Kidney Bean	O_3	2.66	0.114
Tobacco	O_3	1.66	0.145

SOURCE: Lesser et al. (1990).

where: (H/Pop) = ratio of persons with health state (H) to total population (Pop)
α, β, γ = statistically estimated parameters
C = ambient concentration of pollutant
X = factors associated with incidence of health state: age, income, personal habits (smoking, for example)
ε = stochastic term

Exponentiating both sides of the equation and multiplying through by population yields the estimate of the number of persons with a particular health state.[3]

$$(H) = Pop\ (exp^{(\alpha + \gamma X + \beta C)})$$ (3.5)

Agriculture. APEEP uses dose-response functions for agricultural crops from the National Crop Loss Assessment Network (Lesser et al. 1990). Using the coefficients in table 3-2, the dose-response functions take the following form:

$$CY^* = \left(1 - e^{-\left(\frac{O_3}{\sigma}\right)^\gamma}\right) \times CY^b$$ (3.6)

---

3. The functional form in (3.5) is generalized so that readers can easily see the link between (3.4) and (3.5). The specification used for log-linear dose-response models in APEEP is $Pop(1 - (exp^{(\alpha + \gamma X + \beta C)})^{-1})$.

where: CY^* = new crop yield after emissions perturbation
CY^b = baseline crop yield
O_3 = 7- or 12-hour daily mean O_3 concentrations (ppmv)
γ, σ = statistically estimated parameters

The model then calculates the relative yield loss (RYL).

$$RYL = 1 - \left(\frac{CY^*}{CY^b}\right) \tag{3.7}$$

Man-made Materials. Dose-response functions for man-made materials damages are obtained from the NAPAP studies (Atteraas and Haagenrud 1982; Baedecker 1990; Haynie, Spence, and Lipfert 1989) and from more recent experiments conducted by the International Cooperative Programme on Effects on Materials (ICP, 2012). The materials corrosion dose-response functions assume three slightly different forms.

The function representing the effect of ambient SO_2 on galvanized steel is:

$$\Delta M = (\beta_0 SO_2 + \beta_1) \times M \tag{3.8}$$

where: ΔM = mass loss of material
β_0, β_1 = parameters from table 3-3
SO_2 = ambient concentration of pollutant
M = existing material mass

The function representing the effect of ambient SO_2 on painted surfaces includes terms for surface wetness and annual rainfall:

$$\Delta M = \beta_0 R + \beta_1 SO_2 \times Freq \tag{3.9}$$

TABLE 3-3
DOSE-RESPONSE PARAMETERS FOR SO_2 AND MAN-MADE MATERIALS

Material	Source	β_0	β_1
Galvanized Steel	Atteraas and Haagenrud 1982	6.05	0.22
Painted Surfaces	ICP 2012	3.22×10^{-5}	6.0×10^{-3}
Carbonate Stone	ICP 2012	2.7	1.9×10^{-2}

where: ΔM = mass loss of material
β_0, β_1 = parameters from table 2-3
SO_2 = ambient concentration of pollutant
$Freq$ = fraction of time surface is wet
R = annual rainfall (cm)

The function representing the effect of ambient SO_2 on carbonate stone surfaces is:

$$\Delta S = (\beta_0\ SO_2^\kappa exp^{(\gamma T)}) + (\beta_1 R)H^+ \qquad (3.10)$$

where: ΔS = surface recession of painted surface (μm)
β_0, β_1, κ, γ, = statistically estimated parameters
SO_2 = ambient concentration of pollutant
T = ambient temperature (C°)
R= annual rainfall (mm)
H^+ = hydrogen$^+$ concentration of precipitation (mg/L)

The parameters for each of these functions have been empirically estimated in the studies cited in table 3-3.

Timber. The effect of O_3 concentrations on tree growth is assumed to be linear (Reich 1987; Pye 1988). For both deciduous and coniferous species, the dose-response function that APEEP uses is:

$$\Delta Y_m = (\beta_m \Delta O_3) \times G \qquad (3.11)$$

where: ΔY_m = change in timber growth of species m (bft³)
β_m = 0.0015 for coniferous and 0.0065 for deciduous trees
G = baseline timber growth (bft³/yr)
ΔO_3 = change from baseline O_3 (ppm-hour)

Visibility. APEEP uses an empirical model that describes the visual range in each county as a function of climatic and geographical factors and ambient concentrations of PM_{10}. An off-line regression model estimates the empirical relationship between the log of visual range (observations from

U.S. National Oceanic and Atmospheric Administration 2000) and PM_{10} (observations from the USEPA's AIRS network) and other control variables, such as temperature, precipitation, latitude, longitude, and altitude. The components of the regression model are based on the fundamental principles of atmospheric chemistry and physics pertaining to visibility (Seinfeld and Pandis 1998).

The underlying model assumes that visual range (VR) is an exponential function of $PM_{2.5}$ and PM_{10} as well as climate and geography:

$$VR = exp^{(\beta + \gamma C + \delta G + \theta PM + \varepsilon)} \qquad (3.12)$$

where: VR = baseline visual range (miles)
$\theta, \beta, \gamma, \delta$ = statistically estimated parameters
C = county climate data (temperature, precipitation)
G = county geographical data (latitude, longitude, altitude)
PM = county baseline PM_{10} and $PM_{2.5}$ concentration[4]
ε = stochastic term

The coefficient in the regression model for pollution measures the sensitivity of visibility to PM concentrations. The parameter θ is equal to 0.4. Therefore, a 10 percent change in PM will lead to a 4 percent change in VR. The regression model serves as a dose-response function for visibility, relating an incremental change in PM_{10} levels to changes in visibility.

Recreation. APEEP's measure of the dose-response relationship between recreation and exposures to air pollution has two components: a link between SO_2, O_3, NO_x, and forest mortality (FM), and a link between forest mortality and recreation. The forest mortality dose-response function is a linear combination of three air pollutants (SO_2, O_3, and NO_x):

$$FM = \alpha + \beta_1 SO_2 + \beta_2 O_3 + \beta_3 NO_x + \beta_4 G \qquad (3.13)$$

where: FM = forest mortality (ft³)

---

4. The definition of PM_{10} is all particles between 2.5 and 10 microns. By adding PM_{10} and $PM_{2.5}$, the model is capturing all changes in particulates less than 10 microns in size.

α, β = estimated parameters
G = geographic variables: county population, latitude, longitude, altitude, land area
SO_2, O_3, NO_x = ambient concentration (ppbv)

TABLE 3-4
RECREATION AND FOREST MORTALITY PARAMETERS

Pollutant	$SO_2(\beta_1)$	$NO_x(\beta_3)$	$O_3(\beta_2)$	FM
Impact on Forest Mortality	3.3×10^4	1.9×10^5	1.7×10^5	-3.8×10^{-5}

The parameters employed in equations (3.13) and (3.14) are shown in table 3-4.

The link between RVD and forest mortality is also assumed to be linear. In addition to mortality, RVD is expected to depend on the volume of the trees and climate:

$$RVD = \beta_0 + \beta_1 FM + \beta_2 C + \beta_3 V \qquad (3.14)$$

where: RVD = recreation visitor days[5]
FM = forest mortality (ft³) from equation (3.15)
β = estimated parameters
C = climate: annual average temperature (°F), precipitation (in)
V = volume (bft)

Valuation

We have described how APEEP calculates exposures to pollution and translates those exposures into physical effects. The final component of APEEP is the valuation of those effects. The valuation module translates physical effects estimated in the dose-response module into equivalent dollar damages (measured in year 2000 US dollars). Individual readers may prefer to

---

5. RVDs are the total visits to national parks, state parks, national forests, state forests, and Bureau of Land Management land holdings.

use alternative values. APEEP's disaggregated structure makes changing parameters in the valuation module straightforward to do.

We rely on market prices to value goods traded in organized markets (e.g., crops and timber). It is a basic premise of microeconomics that market prices are a useful measure of the marginal value of commodities traded in organized markets. If markets are functioning efficiently, market prices reflect both the marginal cost of producing a market good and the marginal benefit that consumers derive from consumption of that good.

We rely on findings reported in studies from the nonmarket valuation literature in economics for the marginal values associated with nonmarket goods and services. The valuation of nonmarket goods and services, such as visibility, ecosystem services, and especially human health, is more difficult than the application of market prices to value timber and crop yields. However, environmental economists have developed many methods to measure the marginal value of nonmarket goods (see reviews by Freeman 2003; Mendelsohn and Olmstead 2009). In the nonmarket valuation literature, economists frequently distinguish between revealed preference and stated preference methods (Freeman 2003; Mendelsohn and Olmstead 2009). Revealed preference methods use behavior in markets to infer what values people hold. Stated preference methods use surveys to ask people directly about their values. Both methods strive to value the trade-off, at the margin, between a nonmarket good (health or environmental quality, for example) and income (Mendelsohn and Olmstead 2009).

In applying valuation techniques to air pollution impacts, one must consider the time horizon of the impacts. For impacts in the current year, current prices and shadow prices can be used. However, if impacts occur in the future, the values must be discounted back to the year of emission. For example, with timber resources, the model computes the present value of changes to the inventory due to an emission today. For materials, the model estimates the present value of changes in the maintenance schedule.

Human Health. Human health effects associated with ambient pollution levels are commonly divided into two broad categories: premature mortalities and increased incidence rates of morbidity or illness. Prior studies indicate that the bulk of air pollution damages are related to human health (Mendelsohn 1980; USEPA 1999; Muller and Mendelsohn 2007). We consequently provide a detailed review of how mortality and morbidity are valued in this model.

In the default approach to mortality risk valuation, APEEP uses the value of mortality risks that is measured by estimating the relationship between wages and mortality risks faced by workers in the labor market. Specifically, APEEP uses the findings from Mrozek and Taylor, who report a value of mortality risks on the order of $200 per 1/10,000 chance of death (Mrozek and Taylor 2002). In revealed preference studies, the observed wages are regressed on occupational mortality risks and a number of control variables that explain wage rates (see reviews by USEPA 1999; Viscusi and Aldy 2003; Mrozek and Taylor 2002). This is a revealed preference approach, because it uses actual wage and risk data from the marketplace. There are numerous analyses that focus on estimating the trade-off between money and mortality risks. There are many examples of studies that employ revealed preference techniques and many that rely on stated preference approaches. Taken together, the studies suggest a range of mortality risk values of between approximately $200–$1,000 for a small (1/10,000) chance of death. The USEPA has selected a mortality value of $620 per 1/10,000 chance of death for use in its cost-benefit analyses.

In the default valuation scenario used throughout this book, the value of mortality risks is tailored to the age of exposed people using the following formula:

$$V_{ac} = \sum_{t=0}^{T_{ac}} (R\Gamma_{Tac}(1 + \delta)^{-1}) \tag{3.15}$$

where: V_a = present value of a premature mortality of person in age-cohort (a) in county (c)
R = annual mortality risk premium ($/life-year).
T_a = the number of life-years remaining for persons in age-cohort (a) in county (c)
Γ_T = cumulative probability of survival to period (T) for age-cohort (a) living in county (c)
δ = discount rate on life-years

The approach that values life-years remaining places a relatively large value on younger populations relative to older populations because young people have many more life-years remaining. This difference is important for modeling air pollution mortality impacts, because air pollution affects mortality rates in a manner that is proportional to baseline rates, which are considerably larger in older people. We test alternative approaches to mortality valuation in chapter 8.

Some readers may think it is ethically objectionable to affix a dollar value to health effects such as illnesses or death. However, the values discussed above reflect a trade-off between small changes to mortality risks and money that people commonly make in their everyday lives. By buying or not buying products that reduce the risk of death and injury, such as bicycle helmets, bottled water, smoke detectors, and child seats in automobiles, people are revealing the values they hold for small mortality risks. Every regulatory decision related to pollution control that involves a small change to mortality risk implicitly makes a judgment about the value of life. The revealed and stated preference studies estimate the value that society has chosen. Current policy, by consciously ignoring these studies, makes this implicit value decision randomly. As a result, it is often the case that a different value of life is implied by each regulatory decision. This is an inefficient way to reduce mortality risks because it leads to a lot of money being spent to protect a life in some policies and very little in others. Looking across all these decisions, we see that more lives could be saved with the same total abatement expenditure if a single value of mortality risks was used in every regulatory decision.

The value for cases of chronic bronchitis and chronic asthma come from stated preference studies that ask survey respondents how much they would be willing to pay to avoid a case of these two illnesses (USEPA 1999). The remaining valuation estimates for morbidity cases rely on cost-of-illness estimates. Cost of illness is defined as medical expenses plus lost wages. The default value for each health effect is reported in table 3-5.

Agriculture and Commercial Timber. The values for agriculture and timber are derived from market prices. The average 2002 crop price data are obtained from the U.S. Department of Agriculture National Agricultural Statistics Service. The prices are reported in table 3-6.

The 2002 market prices for timber are calculated by region and by timber type (hardwood or softwood). The price data are obtained from Sohngen

TABLE 3-5
VALUE OF HEALTH IMPACTS

Health Event	Unit	Value ($)
Premature Death	Case	1,980,000
Chronic Bronchitis	Case	320,000
Chronic Asthma	Case	30,800
General Respiratory	Hospital Admission	8,300
General Cardiac	Hospital Admission	17,526
Asthma	Hospital Admission	6,700
Chronic Obstructive Pulmonary Disease	Hospital Admission	11,276
Ischemic Heart Disease	Hospital Admission	18,210
Asthma	Emergency Room Visit	240

NOTE: Chapter 8 tests the importance of using $6 million as an alternative value for mortality. Chapters 9 and 10 employ this alternative value for mortality.

TABLE 3-6
AGRICULTURAL CROP PRICES, 2002

Crop	Price ($)	Unit
Corn	2.25	Bushel
Cotton	0.61	Lbs.
Peanut	0.17	Lbs.
Grain Sorghum	4.13	Cwt.
Soybeans	5.19	Bushel
Spring Wheat	3.42	Bushel
Alfalfa	108.36	Ton
Tobacco	1.86	Lbs.
Dry Beans	6.82	Cwt.

SOURCE: U.S. Department of Agriculture 2002.

and Mendelsohn 1998. The prices reflect the value of standing timber in 2002 (not delivered logs). These market prices are reported in table 3-7.

The timing of future timber harvests is determined by maximizing the net present value of timber stock (Faustmann 1849). In the formula shown below, (t) corresponds to the rotation that maximizes the present value of timber stocks. This optimal harvest age varies according to major species groups and region:

TABLE 3-7
COMMERCIAL TIMBER PRICES, 2002

Region	Timber Type	$/thousand board feet
Northeast	Hardwood	275
Northeast	Softwood	90
Southeast	Hardwood	270
Southeast	Softwood	312
West	Softwood	462
Midwest	Hardwood	275
Midwest	Softwood	90

SOURCE: Sohngen and Mendelsohn 1998.

$$W_r = (PQ_{tr}e^{-\delta} - Ce^{-\delta})/(1-e^{-\delta}) \qquad (3.16)$$

where: W_r = present value of timber in receptor county (r)
P = 2002 price for timber ($/thousand board feet, denoted MBF)
Q_{tr} = volume of timber (MBF) in time (t) in receptor county (r)
δ = market interest rate (4%)
C = replanting costs ($/MBF)
t = time of harvest

NO_x and VOC emissions are expected to cause O_3 concentrations to increase, which slow forest growth. This will affect both the size of trees at harvest, Q, and the length of forest rotations, t. The APEEP model compares W_r given different emission scenarios that correspond to different O_3 concentrations and exposures.

Man-made Materials. The dose-response model predicts the loss of materials from pollution. As pollution reduces material lifetime, it reduces the time interval between repairs. If we assume that maintenance is performed to replace lost materials; the damage from the pollution is the increased present value of maintenance costs associated with doing maintenance more often. This may be an overestimate of the damages if the material outlasts the economic usefulness of the building. For example, if stone building materials last for 1,000 years, but the building will be in use for only 100 years, the decay in the stone might not have any value. However, for more short-lived assets, such as painted surfaces, the present value of maintenance is likely to be an accurate valuation. The annual cost of having a higher present value of maintenance is:

$$Maintenance_r = \delta\left(\frac{RC_r e^{-\delta t}}{1 - e^{-\delta t}}\right) \tag{3.17}$$

where: $Maintenance_r$ = annual maintenance costs in county (r)
δ = market interest rate (4%)
RC_r = replacement costs in receptor county (r)
t = time interval between repairs

The annual cost of the material damage is the interest rate times the change in the present value of the maintenance schedules. The APEEP model compares maintenance costs, given different emission scenarios corresponding to differing SO_2 concentrations and exposures.

Visibility. Several studies use contingent valuation (stated preference) to derive estimates of the value of visibility (Chestnut and Rowe 1990; Loehman and Boldt 1990; McClelland et al. 1993). The studies show respondents pictures of the same landscape with different visual range and ask how much they would value a clearer day. We rely on Chestnut and Rowe's (1990) estimates of household willingness to pay (HHWTP) for incremental changes in visibility associated with recreation experiences.

$$HHWTP = \beta \times \left(ln\left(\frac{VR1}{VR2}\right)\right) \tag{3.18}$$

where: $HHWTP$ = household willingness to pay
β = statistically estimated parameter
$VR2$ = visual range (miles) after emissions perturbation
$VR1$ = visual range (miles) under baseline conditions

The values of visibility are reported in table 3-8. The model employs regional estimates of HHWTP for improvements in residential and recreational visibility (Chestnut and Rowe 1990; McClelland et al. 1993).

TABLE 3-8

VALUE OF VISIBILITY

Visibility Being Valued	Value ($)	Location	Source
In-Region Recreation	170	Southwest	Chestnut and Rowe (1990)
Out-of-Region Recreation	135	Southwest	Chestnut and Rowe (1990)
In-Region Recreation	80	Southeast	Chestnut and Rowe (1990)
Out-of-Region Recreation	50	Southeast	Chestnut and Rowe (1990)
In-Region Residential	174	Eastern	McClelland et al. (1993)

Recreation. Recreation is valued using travel cost and contingent valuation methods. In particular, we use an average value for recreation in forest ecosystems from a United Nations Food and Agriculture Organization report (Kengen 1997). The value of $62.80 is used for each RVD in forest environments. The estimate averages the value of hiking, camping, and hunting days.

4

Calculating the Marginal Damages of Air Pollution

This study is not the first to use an integrated assessment model to value air pollution damage (e.g., Mendelsohn 1980; USEPA 1999; Fann et al. 2009; Levy et al. 2009). The critical contribution of this research is that we use the IAM to calculate the marginal damage from emissions. Past researchers have generally used IAMs to calculate aggregate damages of national policies, although in some papers the models have been used to examine a single source of emissions (Mendelsohn 1980; Fann et al. 2009; Levy et al. 2009). For example, the USEPA used an IAM to calculate the value of the total reduction of emissions that resulted from the implementation of the Clean Air Act (USEPA 1999). Aggregate analyses can discern the overall effect of a set of regulations such as the Clean Air Act. However, aggregated analyses cannot discern the merits of particular aspects of the act. Specifically, such analyses cannot discern whether the regulations have properly weighed the costs and benefits of each pollutant and whether the regulations are efficiently managing each source. To evaluate whether or not the Clean Air Act can be improved, one needs to determine the marginal damage of emissions. Then, by comparing the marginal damage to the marginal cost of each emission, one can evaluate whether the regulations are efficient.

There are many applications of this basic principle. How efficient are different pieces of the Clean Air Act legislation? How efficient is the regulation of each pollutant? How does the regulation of a specific pollutant compare across industries? How does the regulation of a specific pollutant compare across sources in different locations? By calculating source-specific marginal damages, one can answer these additional questions and explore the details of pollution management. This is illustrated quite clearly in the remaining chapters.

The computation of marginal damages in this chapter shows that damage per ton varies on many levels. First, the analysis reveals quite clearly that the marginal damage of each pollutant is not the same. Tons of sulfur dioxide should not be traded with tons of nitrogen dioxide. They do not cause the same damage. Second, we find great variability in marginal damages *for the same pollutant* emitted in different places. While Fann et al. (2009) and Levy et al. (2009) also found evidence of such heterogeneity, the modeling conducted in this analysis is distinct from their work in two ways. First, Fann et al. (2009) compute damages per ton for a relatively small sample of sites, whereas the current work covers nearly 10,000 sources over the entire United States. Second, Levy et al. (2009) focus entirely on coal-fired power plants. In contrast, the current work covers many different source types, *in addition to* coal-fired power plants. Hence, source location is also important. Within every state, we find that the impact per ton of emissions varies dramatically depending on whether the emission occurs in a city or a rural area. Urban emissions are far more harmful than rural emissions. In order to achieve efficiency, regulations must treat such discharges differently. Marginal damage analysis reveals these important insights to regulators, whereas analyses that employ state average damages per ton may fail to see the importance of source location.

Our research calculates the marginal damage of emissions one source and one pollutant at a time, and in doing so, it isolates the source-specific marginal damages of emissions. This approach reveals important insights for more efficient regulatory design across industry, across pollutants, and across space. By producing marginal damage estimates, we provide regulators with data that may be used to design efficient pollution policy, as described in chapter 1.

Marginal Damage Algorithm

In the first step toward computing marginal damages, APEEP relies on the baseline estimates of emissions in the United States for the year 2002 calculated and reported by the USEPA (USEPA, 2006). In its national emission inventory, the USEPA aggregates many small sources to the county level. For many individually monitored stationary sources, the USEPA reports emissions by source. Combining the aggregated county-level sources with the individual point sources leads to a total of ten thousand distinct sources. Each of these ten thousand sources is treated separately by APEEP.

The algorithm to estimate marginal damages at these ten thousand sources begins with a single run for all the sources simultaneously producing their baseline emission levels of all pollutants to calculate baseline damage. The second step in the algorithm adds one ton of one pollutant to one source. National damages are computed with this additional ton. The marginal damage of that ton is the difference in the national damages before and after the ton is added to baseline emissions. By holding emissions of all other sources at their baseline levels, the algorithm isolates the contribution of a single ton of emissions at each source to total (national) damages.

Note that the marginal damage algorithm captures the impact the ton of emission has on all county receptor locations in the contiguous United States. The impact is not limited to the county where the emission occurs. Note also that the calculation includes the impact of secondary pollutants created as a result of the one ton of emission. APEEP ascribes the damage due to secondary pollutants to the source of emissions. For example, emissions of SO_2 contribute to the formation of ammonium sulfate, an important constituent of $PM_{2.5}$ and PM_{10}. When a ton of SO_2 is added to a particular source in APEEP, the damages resulting from the increase in $PM_{2.5}$ and PM_{10} are attributed back to the emission of SO_2 at the selected source. The marginal damage (MD) of an emission from origin (j) of pollutant (s) is the sum of the change in damages across the complete set (R) of receptor counties:

$$MD_{s,j} = \sum_r (D_r(X_{1,s})) - \sum_r (D_r(X_{0,s})) \qquad (4.1)$$

where: D_r = total dollar damage in receptor county (r)
$X_{0,s}$ = baseline emissions of pollutant (s)
$X_{1,s}$ = baseline emissions of pollutant (s) plus one ton from source (j)

The summation could potentially include every county in the United States, but many counties are too far away (or located upwind) to be affected by emissions from particular sources. The model sums the increase in damage across the receptor counties where concentrations of pollution actually change as a result of the marginal emission.

After computing the marginal damage of emissions for a specific pollutant from source (j), we repeat this experiment for each of the six pollutants covered in this book and the approximately ten thousand distinct (individual and grouped) sources in the United States. The total ten thousand sources encompass all reported anthropogenic emissions of these six pollutants in the lower forty-eight states. Estimating the complete set of marginal damages requires sixty thousand repetitions of the experiment outlined above (ten thousand sources times the six pollutants). Computationally, the APEEP model achieves this arduous series of tasks through the use of the reduced-form air quality modeling apparatus that is described in chapter 2. This approach reduces the calculation to a series of linear algebraic operations that are easy for modern matrix software to execute. Chapter 5 extends this relatively simple algorithm to encompass statistical uncertainty in the various stages of the APEEP model.

The algorithm is used to calculate annual marginal damages (Muller and Mendelsohn 2007; 2009; Muller, Mendelsohn, and Nordhaus 2011). The analysis could be extended to examine intra-annual differences that focus on seasonal, or even daily, changes in marginal damages. For example, the marginal impact of NO_x and VOCs depend on temperature as well as biogenic emissions of many compounds. An example of biogenic emissions includes the fact that softwood, coniferous trees emit VOCs. As a result of these and other meteorological factors, the processes involved with atmospheric chemistry may change the marginal damage per ton of these pollutants from day to day. More specifically, the marginal damage of each of the criteria pollutants covered by APEEP depends on how they are physically dispersed throughout the lower levels of the atmosphere. Because weather is variable, marginal damages will also vary on a daily basis. APEEP is not designed to take into account these daily fluctuations. That is, the model is calibrated to use annual, and for the case of O_3 formation, seasonal, average meteorological conditions associated with each source and receptor location in the United States. Therefore, the model by construction cannot predict what the actual marginal damage is on a given day. However, the Air Pollution Impact Model (Tong et al. 2006) could make these intra-annual calculations because it is constructed to run real-time simulations capitalizing on observed weather conditions in particular locations that have not been averaged. Using such a tool, future researchers could explore how marginal damages vary by season, month, or even day.

Results

The first set of results in chapter 4 explores the statistical distribution of the marginal damages for each of the six pollutants listed above across all sources in the contiguous United States. These results consist of the marginal damages from all of the nearly ten thousand sources in the United States for each of the six air pollutants covered in this study.[1]

Table 4-1 reports the quantiles from the distributions of the resulting marginal damages. The median (50th percentile) marginal damages of emissions for NH_3 is approximately $1,500 (per ton); for SO_2 the median source generates $1,640 in damage per ton; and for $PM_{2.5}$, the median is just over $2,000 per ton. In contrast, the median marginal damages of emissions for PM_{10}, NO_x, and VOCs are much smaller in magnitude. For PM_{10} the median marginal damage is just $190 per ton; for VOC the median is $240/ton; and for NO_x the damage per ton from the median source is approximately $370. Hence, table 4-1 indicates that NH_3, SO_2, and $PM_{2.5}$ emissions are far more dangerous per ton than PM_{10}, NO_x, and VOCs.

Table 4-1 indicates that the marginal damages of emissions vary a great deal across all sources in the United States. The range of marginal damages is greatest for NH_3 and $PM_{2.5}$. Marginal damages for $PM_{2.5}$ range from $480/ton in the lowest percentile to $68,810/ton in the highest (99.9th) percentile. This is a difference of a factor of over 100. The range for NH_3 is from $150/ton to $84,530/ton. This is a difference of a factor of over 500. The variability in the distributions of damages for $PM_{2.5}$ and NH_3 highlight the importance of modeling *source-specific* damages; when used to inform policy design, such damages suggest placing a greater priority on abatement of emissions generated by sources in the 99.9th percentile than from sources toward the 1st percentile, *ceteris paribus*. In contrast, the range for NO_x is between $170/ton and $2,580/ton.

---

1. The sixty thousand marginal damages (six pollutants for each source) are available under AP2 Data at the following website: https://sites.google.com/site/nickmullershomepage/home/ap2-data. (Muller, 2012)

TABLE 4-1

MARGINAL DAMAGES OF EMISSIONS BY PERCENTILE ($/TON/YEAR)

Pollutant	1st%	25th%	50th%	75th%	99th%	99.9th%	E[MD]*
$PM_{2.5}$	480	1,270	2,090	3,490	20,340	68,810	5,390
PM_{10}	60	130	190	310	2,080	6,660	450
NO_x	170	230	370	560	1,250	2,580	380
NH_3	150	480	1,460	3,330	33,220	84,530	3,940
VOC	60	150	240	390	2,120	7,040	1,090
SO_2	360	920	1,640	2,150	6,380	15,780	2,060

*The final column is the expected marginal damage of emissions for each pollutant in the United States. The expectation in this context is an emission-weighted average across the distribution of marginal damages for each pollutant, and it is shown in equation (4.2).

Table 4-1 also reveals that the distribution of marginal damages is right-skewed. The marginal damages of the 99th percentile source minus the 50th percentile source (median) is significantly larger than the difference between the marginal damage of the 50th percentile source and the 1st percentile source. The right-skewed property of the distributions explains why the expected marginal damages are higher than the median marginal damages. The expected value of the marginal damages for each pollutant is the emission-weighted average of the marginal damages across all sources (j):

$$E[MD_s] = \sum_j \left(\frac{MD_{s,j}X_{s,j}}{\sum_j X_{j,s}} \right)$$ (4.2)

where: $E[\ ]$ = expectation operator
$MD_{s,j}$ = marginal damage of emissions of pollutant (s) from source (j)
$X_{s,j}$ = emissions of pollutant (s) from source (j)

The expected value of the marginal damages of $PM_{2.5}$, PM_{10}, NH_3, and VOC are more than twice as large as their median value. This finding suggests that large amounts of emissions of these pollutants are produced by sources that also generate high marginal damages. In equation (4.2), sources that produce large amounts of emissions are given greater weight than those producing a relatively small amount of tonnage. For a pollutant such as SO_2, large quantities of emissions are produced by power plants in the rural

FIGURE 4-1
MARGINAL DAMAGE OF PM₂.₅ EMISSIONS ($/TON/YEAR)

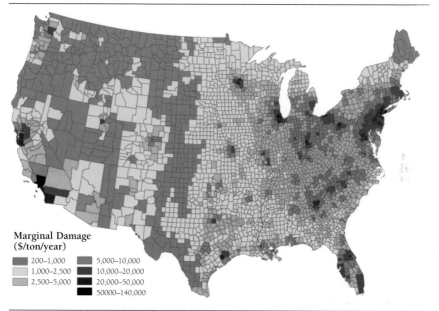

Marginal Damage
($/ton/year)

200–1,000	5,000–10,000
1,000–2,500	10,000–20,000
2,500–5,000	20,000–50,000
	50000–140,000

SOURCE: Muller and Mendelsohn 2009.

Midwest, where marginal damages tend to be low. As a result, the expected value is just 1.3 times larger than the median source. Mapping the results shows how the marginal damages vary across space. Figure 4-1 displays the marginal damage due to ground-level emissions of PM₂.₅ from all counties in the contiguous United States. Ground-level emissions are produced by mobile sources, residential sources, and industrial or commercial facilities without a tall smokestack. The figure reveals that the marginal damages vary a great deal across space. Every metropolitan area is highlighted by the map as a relatively harmful place to emit PM₂.₅. This is because emissions in these locations lead to high human exposures and thus harmful human health effects. The rural West, in contrast, has noticeably lower marginal damages because of its low population density.

Sources in the lower percentiles of the distribution are mostly in the rural areas in the western United States, such as the Rocky Mountain and Great Plains states. Sources with median marginal damages of emissions (close to the 50th percentile) are found mostly in eastern states as well as

FIGURE 4-2
MARGINAL DAMAGE OF SO$_2$ EMISSIONS ($/TON/YEAR)

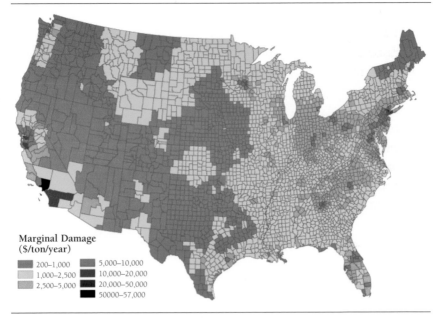

Marginal Damage
($/ton/year)

- 200–1,000
- 1,000–2,500
- 2,500–5,000
- 5,000–10,000
- 10,000–20,000
- 20,000–50,000
- 50000–57,000

SOURCE: Muller and Mendelsohn 2009.

in suburban and small urban areas. Sources whose emissions produce the highest marginal damages are located in the metropolitan counties.

Figure 4-2 displays the marginal damages of SO$_2$. The map resembles the results for PM$_{2.5}$ except that the marginal damages are generally lower and the differences among localities are not as great. SO$_2$ is not as harmful in metropolitan areas because it takes time for the SO$_2$ to form ammonium sulfate, which is an important constituent of PM$_{2.5}$. Moreover, only after SO$_2$ has contributed to concentrations of PM$_{2.5}$ does it become most harmful. The result is that the marginal damages shown in figure 4-2 are more uniform across space compared to those shown in figure 4-1. Despite this difference, the predominant theme evident in figure 4-2 is that emissions of SO$_2$ in urban areas are more harmful, ton for ton, than emissions in more rural locales.

Figure 4-3 shows the marginal damage of emissions for NH$_3$ that interact with NO$_x$ and especially SO$_2$ in the atmosphere to form PM$_{2.5}$. The relative harm of an emission of NH$_3$ is dictated by the ambient concentrations of both NO$_x$ and SO$_2$. Generally, such concentrations are higher in cities and in the eastern United

FIGURE 4-3
MARGINAL DAMAGE OF NH_3 EMISSIONS (\$/TON/YEAR)

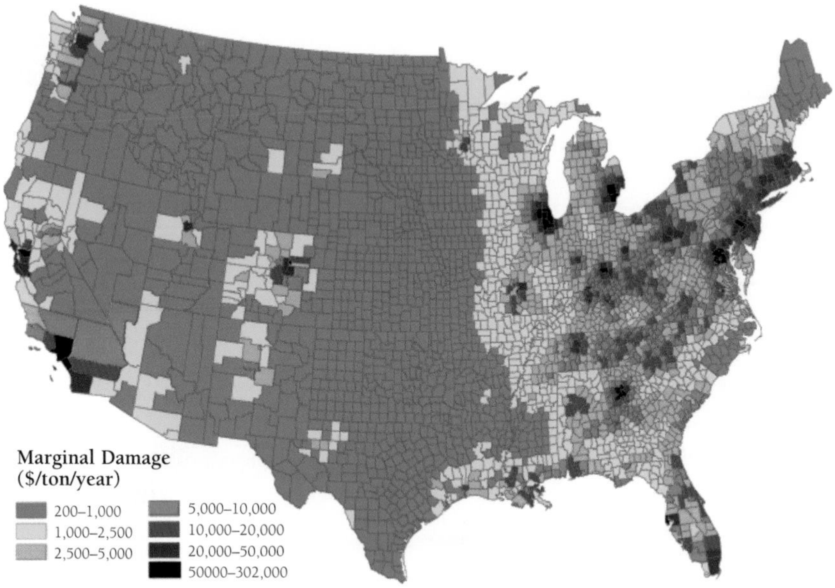

Marginal Damage
(\$/ton/year)

■ 200–1,000	■ 5,000–10,000
▢ 1,000–2,500	■ 10,000–20,000
▢ 2,500–5,000	■ 20,000–50,000
	■ 50000–302,000

SOURCE: Muller and Mendelsohn 2009.

States. The relatively high marginal damages of emissions for NH_3 in urban areas and in counties east of the Mississippi River are due to *both* the higher population densities near these sources and the background presence of both NO_x and SO_2.

Figure 4-4 displays the marginal damages of emissions for NO_x that contribute to ambient concentrations of O_3, and they combine with NH_3 to form ammonium nitrate, a component of $PM_{2.5}$. Figure 4-4 shows that the marginal damage of NO_x emissions tends to be higher in cities, but there is a distinct area in the central United States where damages per ton of emissions are also elevated. This is because copious amounts of NH_3 from agricultural sources are present in this region, which, when combined with emitted NO_x, lead to higher concentration of $PM_{2.5}$.

Certain counties in densely populated metropolitan areas show negative NO_x marginal damages: additional tons are beneficial. This result stems from nonlinear chemical reactions between and among VOCs and NO_x involved with the formation of tropospheric O_3 (see Seinfeld and Pandis 1998; Muller and Mendelsohn 2012).

FIGURE 4-4

MARGINAL DAMAGE OF NO$_x$ EMISSIONS ($/TON/YEAR)

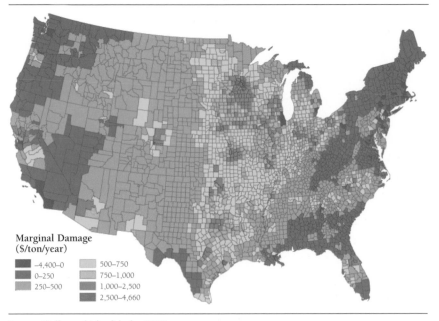

Marginal Damage
($/ton/year)

■ −4,400–0	□ 500–750
■ 0–250	▨ 750–1,000
▨ 250–500	■ 1,000–2,500
	■ 2,500–4,660

SOURCE: Muller and Mendelsohn 2009.

The calculation of marginal damages used in this book is based on reported baseline emissions in 2002. As baseline emissions change over time, marginal damages must be recalculated. For example, if regulations were relaxed and emissions grew substantially, the marginal damages would likely increase. On the other hand, if regulations were tightened and emissions fell substantially, the marginal damages would likely decrease. The calculation of marginal damages is also sensitive to the underlying population levels and income associated with the baseline conditions. If population increases through time, the damages will increase because more people will be exposed to subsequent emissions. Similarly, as incomes rise, the damages will increase because each recipient will be willing to pay more to avoid the risks associated with pollution exposure. This sensitivity to socioeconomic changes suggests that the marginal damage estimates should be updated regularly, perhaps every ten years, with data provided by the U.S. Census. The marginal damages reported in this chapter form the basis of much of the empirical and policy analysis in subsequent chapters of this book.

5

Statistical Uncertainty

In this chapter, we explore the uncertainty associated with estimating the marginal damages that are reported in chapter 4. The analysis conducted in this chapter is important for two reasons. First, policymakers may want to know the uncertainty of the damage estimates used to design efficient regulations or to conduct damage assessments. In essence, regulators need to know how precise, or imprecise, the damage estimates are before a serious consideration of their use in designing or evaluating policy. Second, uncertainty analysis is important as a guide to researchers who can do further studies to reduce the uncertainty of any single parameter or element in the analysis.[1]

Generally, three types of uncertainty potentially impact the marginal damage estimates: model uncertainty, input uncertainty, and parameter uncertainty. Model uncertainty reflects the manner in which a particular model emulates, mimics, and ultimately captures a process. In the present context, modeling uncertainty relates to the linkages between emissions, concentrations, exposures, physical effects, and monetary damages. Do these linkages reflect the way in which air pollution emissions affect sensitive populations? Are the functional forms correct? Are important mechanisms captured? Are critical aspects of this process accurately represented by the model? These questions and concerns focus on model uncertainty. Although model uncertainty is important, it is difficult to quantify. In the following analysis, we focus on input and parameter uncertainty.

It is important to recall that the APEEP model used in this book focuses on the long-run impact of pollution on exposures to annual and seasonal means, not daily or hourly pollution levels. This strategy relies on evidence that exposures to annual and seasonal mean concentrations, as opposed

---

1. The methods used in this chapter are discussed at greater length in Muller 2011.

to impacts on daily mortality rates due to exposures to daily fluctuations in pollution, produce the bulk of air pollution damages (USEPA 1999). Although short-run exposures can also cause damage, the effects due to acute exposure have been shown to be small in magnitude compared to the effects due to long-run, or chronic, exposure. Furthermore, some of the effects of acute exposures are captured by chronic exposures because chronic exposures are just cumulative acute exposures. Is it appropriate to focus solely on long-term concentrations? What bias and error are introduced by omitting acute exposures? The results suggest that the magnitude of damages caused by acute exposures is small. The uncertainty added to the results by omitting short-term exposures and damages is therefore expected to be small as well.

Input uncertainty relates to the data used in the model. Are these data accurate? Are the data measured with error? Are the data sampled from a population? Do the samples represent the population? In the context of air pollution modeling, one critical aspect of input uncertainty is the emissions data. Some emissions data, such as discharges from large point sources, are measured carefully. Emissions from other sources, such as cars and households, are not measured but rather estimated. The uncertainty surrounding the emissions imparts a degree of uncertainty, which is propagated through the modeling chain. This chapter explores input uncertainty by analyzing the impact that imprecision in both emissions data and human population estimates has on the marginal damage estimates.

Parameter uncertainty centers on particular numeric values in the model that govern key aspects of the modeling chain. One important parameter in the model is the sensitivity of adult mortality rates to annual exposures to $PM_{2.5}$. Controlled experiments on serious human health effects such as mortality and severe morbidity are forbidden for ethical reasons. Policy analysis has to rely on natural experiments to explore these relationships. Natural experiments may be flawed due to the inability of researchers to control for possible confounding factors, especially because randomized designs have only begun to be employed in this context. As a result of this and other issues, the estimated parameters from such studies are consequently uncertain. Another important parameter in the IAM is the parameter that measures the monetary value of a change to mortality risk. Differences in the magnitude of this value result from study design, the sample of workers or survey respondents, and the nature of the risks on which the studies focus. Hence, the mortality valuation parameter is also uncertain. Critical questions related to parameter uncertainty include the following: How precise are the estimates of these parameters employed in the model? What impact does the uncertainty in these parameters have on the marginal damage estimates?

Below we explore the influence that the following four parameters have on the marginal damage estimates: estimated annual emissions, county-specific human populations, the sensitivity of mortality rates to exposures, and the value of mortality. The chapter uses Monte Carlo analysis to characterize the cumulative uncertainty in the marginal damages from a small sample of power plants when these four input parameters are modeled stochastically. The analysis explores the relative influence each of these parameters has on the cumulative uncertainty in the damage estimates.

Methods

This uncertainty analysis uses four power plants as a case study. To model the impact of uncertainty associated with estimated annual emissions, county-specific human populations, the sensitivity of mortality to $PM_{2.5}$ exposures, and the value of mortality in APEEP, we use the algorithm for computing marginal damages developed and discussed in chapter 4. This entails running the APEEP model using the baseline emissions (USEPA 2006) for the year 2002 and computing the resulting exposures, mortalities, and monetary damages. Next, one ton of one pollutant is added to a specific source, and the APEEP model is run again. Exposures, mortalities and other effects, and damages are estimated for the augmented emissions. Because the only change between the two computations is the additional ton of pollution, the resulting change in damages is attributed to the change in emissions; it measures the marginal damage.

We now conduct a Monte Carlo analysis using this framework. We assume that each uncertain parameter comes from a normal distribution with known means and variances. Our estimates of the form of the distributions corresponding to emissions, human populations, mortality dose-response, and valuation are all based on peer-reviewed studies and can be derived directly from these studies. The distributions are not arbitrary.

The uncertainty analysis of emissions focuses on emissions from coal-fired power plants measured using the USEPA's Continuous Emission Monitoring System. Although discharges from these sources are measured, there is still measurement error, as reported by researchers in this area (Frey and Zheng 2002; Frey and Li 2003; Abdel-Aziz and Frey 2004; Kuykendal et al. 2006). The estimated ranges of variability in Kuykendal et al. (2006) are used as the basis for the constructed distributions for emissions. Uncertainty in human populations is modeled using estimates of the error in the U.S. Census Bureau's population projections (Stoto 1983). The uncertainty associated with the mortality dose-response is derived from Pope et al. (2002). And the corresponding value of mortality risks is estimated from a meta-analysis covering nearly thirty studies that estimate the value attributed to small changes to mortality risks reported by the USEPA (1999).

The Monte Carlo procedure consists of repeating the following five steps five thousand times for each pollutant species (s) and each location (j):

(1)   Take a random draw from each input distribution.

(2)   Compute the concentration, exposures, physical effects, and monetary damages using APEEP and this specific random draw of parameters.

(3)   Add 1 ton of pollutant species (s) to source (j).

(4)   Recompute the concentrations, exposures, physical effects, and damages given +1 ton of pollutant species (s) at source (j) with the same draws from the distributions in (1).

(5)   Calculate the difference in damages between steps (2) and (4) and assign this marginal damage to pollutant species (s) at source (j).

This case study explores four distinct power plants, one each in Indiana, New York, Texas, and Delaware. The sites were chosen to represent facilities in different regions both in urban and rural locations. The analysis focuses on emissions of two pollutants: SO_2 and $PM_{2.5}$. Because there are five thousand per-ton damage estimates for each pollutant and source, a total of forty thousand iterations were conducted. The resulting model output is an empirical distribution of marginal damages for each facility and

TABLE 5-1

STOCHASTIC AND DETERMINISTIC MARGINAL DAMAGES
OF FOUR POWER PLANTS

Facility	Stochastic		Deterministic	
	Pollutant			
	SO_2	$PM_{2.5}$	SO_2	$PM_{2.5}$
New York	12,160	38,430	12,200	38,860
	(16,990)	(52,970)		
	[1.40]	[1.38]		
Texas	6,290	7,040	6,350	7,100
	(3,890)	(4,540)		
	[0.62]	[0.64]		
Indiana	11,070	12,550	11,260	12,600
	(7,730)	(12,300)		
	[0.70]	[0.98]		
Delaware	15,850	23,160	16,044	23,410
	(11,750)	(26,390)		
	[0.74]	[1.14]		

NOTES: All values are expressed in ($/ton); the stochastic estimates include the expected value of damages, the standard deviation in parentheses, and the coefficients of variation in brackets.

pollutant. Because the same draws from the input distributions are used in steps (2) through (5), the difference in damages is strictly attributable to the additional ton in step (3). Ultimately, these distributions can be used to derive the mean marginal damage and the confidence intervals for marginal damages for power plants. Similar analyses can be done for other sources of pollution and for the remaining four pollutants.

Results

Table 5-1 reports the mean, standard deviations, and coefficient of variation (defined as the standard deviation divided by the mean) for the marginal damage estimates for both SO_2 and $PM_{2.5}$ corresponding to the four fossil fuel–fired power plants. The results indicate that the marginal damage of SO_2 emitted from the power plant in New York has a mean of $12,160, a standard deviation of $16,990, and a coefficient of variation of 1.4. The marginal damage of $PM_{2.5}$ emitted from the same facility has a mean value of

$38,430, a standard deviation of $52,970, and a corresponding coefficient of variation of 1.38. The large degrees of variation (shown in the large standard deviations that are nearly one and one-half times the mean values) suggest that the estimates of the mean marginal damages for this power plant are highly uncertain. This high degree of uncertainty is important for policymakers to acknowledge if they were to employ these damage estimates in cost-benefit analyses or other policy evaluations.

Focusing on the expected value of damage for $PM_{2.5}$ reported in table 5-1, we find that the greatest damage per ton is associated with emissions from the facility in New York and smaller damages for emissions from the plants in Delaware, Indiana, and Texas, in that order. The high concentration of people near the New York plant leads to higher exposures and health effects on a per-ton basis. Looking at the mean damages for SO_2, we see a slightly different pattern. The facility in Delaware generates the greatest damage per ton, with damages then descending for New York, Indiana, and Texas. This result occurs because when SO_2 is emitted, it takes some time (and, spatially, distance if the wind is blowing) before it turns into $PM_{2.5}$. With prevailing southwesterly winds, the emissions in Delaware blow into the New York metropolitan area after the SO_2 has been converted into $PM_{2.5}$. In contrast, some of the SO_2 emissions in New York are transported by prevailing winds out of the metropolitan area before they turn into $PM_{2.5}$. This leads to lower per-ton damage for SO_2 from the New York plant relative to the Delaware plant. An additional pattern in table 5-1 is that the damages due to emissions of $PM_{2.5}$ are uniformly more harmful than emissions of SO_2. This occurs because only a fraction of emitted SO_2 transforms into constituents of $PM_{2.5}$, and, therefore, SO_2 has a smaller effect on health. This particular pattern is also evident in table 4-1.

We present two measures of uncertainty. The standard deviation measures the spread of the distribution of estimated damage from a single source across all the different Monte Carlo runs. The coefficient of variation is the ratio of the standard deviation to the mean; it is a standardized measure of variability. Both measures of uncertainty in the marginal damage distributions follow a distinct spatial pattern. The coefficients of variation are largest for the facility in New York. Even standardizing for the magnitude of damage, we see that the estimates of the damage caused by emissions of SO_2 and $PM_{2.5}$ are most uncertain for the plant in New York. The next largest coefficient of variation corresponds to the plant in Delaware. The plants in Indiana and then Texas have the third and fourth largest coefficients of variation, respectively. The uncertainty in the marginal damage estimates follows a population gradient; sources with larger proximal populations tend to have more uncertain marginal damage estimates. This finding is especially important for policymakers because, as we will show in subsequent chapters, most of the damage from air pollution emissions is associated with sources in cities.

Table 5-1 also indicates that the distributions for PM$_{2.5}$ marginal damages tend to be more uncertain than those corresponding to SO$_2$. That is, the coefficients of variation for PM$_{2.5}$ are larger for each facility except for the plant in New York. Having a sense of whether the damage estimates for specific pollutants are more or less uncertain than estimates for other pollutants is also a critical insight for regulators who often have to manage multiple pollutants under policies such as the Clean Air Act.

Examining the standard deviation of damage reveals that it is large compared to the expected value of damages. Some readers may jump to the conclusion that there is too much error in the marginal damage calculation to regulate pollution. However, efficient policies should not be determined by 95 percent confidence intervals, whether one is talking about the 5 percent level (certain of damage) or the 95 percent level (certain of safety). The optimal regulations should be set at the expected value of damage. Furthermore, the question of whether one should develop regulations based on location does not depend on the absolute value of damages but rather on the relative damages in one location versus another. The uncertainty about the relative damages in one place versus another is much lower, because the great uncertainty surrounding dose response and valuation plays little role in the ratio of damages from place to place.

Table 5-1 also reports the deterministic value of marginal damages when all input parameters are included at their expected value. Each of the deterministic marginal damages for both SO$_2$ and PM$_{2.5}$ is quite similar in magnitude to the mean value of the damage distributions produced by the Monte Carlo procedure. The bias varies from 0.3 percent to 2 percent. We interpret this as being only a relatively small error. The data in table 5-1 suggest that the deterministic value is actually a good measure of the mean marginal damage.

FIGURE 5-1

KERNEL DENSITY GRAPHS: SO$_2$ MARGINAL DAMAGE—FOUR POWER PLANTS

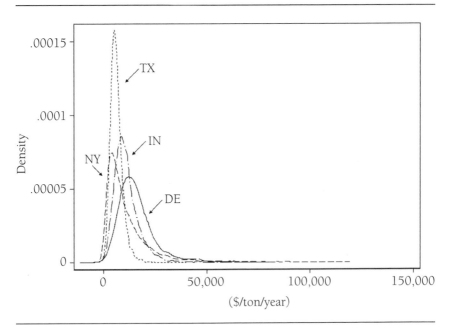

SOURCE: Muller 2011.

All of the marginal damage distributions are characterized by a long right tail. That is, the distributions are right-skewed. This is evident in figures 5-1 and 5-2, which show representations of the distributions of the marginal damages reported in table 5-1. An inspection of these figures shows that the marginal damage distributions have a long right-hand tail; there are relatively few draws from the Monte Carlo procedure that yield very large marginal damage realizations..

Figure 5-1 displays the kernel density graphs (Gaussian kernel) corresponding to the SO$_2$ marginal damage estimates for the four fossil fuel–fired power plants shown in table 5-1. The distributions are right-skewed. As reported in prior research, it is likely that the multiplicative nature of the integrated assessment model drives the right-skewed quality of the damage distributions (Rabl and Spadaro 1999).

Figure 5-2 displays the kernel density graphs corresponding to PM$_{2.5}$ damages for the same four power plants. The right-skewed nature of the

FIGURE 5-2

KERNEL DENSITY GRAPHS: PM$_{2.5}$ MARGINAL DAMAGE—FOUR POWER PLANTS

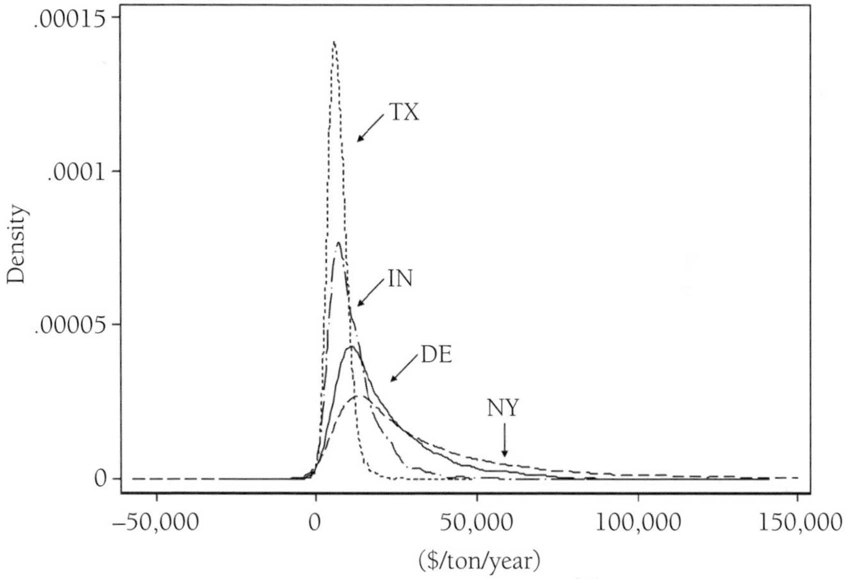

SOURCE: Muller 2011.

distribution is more evident for PM$_{2.5}$. This is especially clear in the New York and Delaware plants.

In Figures 5-3, 5-4, and 5-5, we explore the relationship between the level of damage as dictated by particular realizations from the marginal damage distributions and the spatial extent of the damage. These three figures map the damages over space that are due to an emission of one ton of SO$_2$ from the fossil fuel–fired power plant in Indiana. Figure 5-3 corresponds to the 5th percentile draw. This realization reflects a damage per ton of $2,430, which is considerably smaller than the mean level reported in table 5-1 of $11,070. For this realization, damages are predominantly limited to areas to the north and east of the source location. A few notably impacted metropolitan areas are also marked on the map to provide spatial reference points. Figure 5-4 corresponds to the median, or the 50th percentile, from the SO$_2$ distribution. The damage in this case is approximately $9,400/ton. Note that this value is also smaller than the

FIGURE 5-3
SPATIAL IMPACT OF SO₂ EMISSION FROM POWER PLANT IN INDIANA:
5TH PERCENTILE DRAW

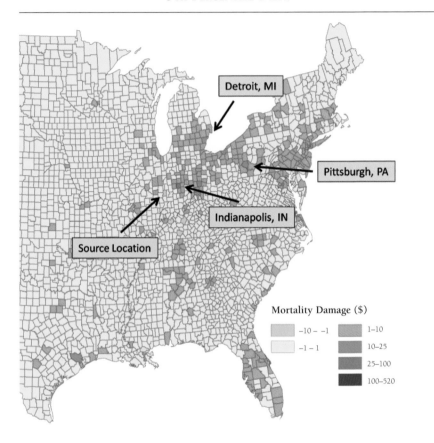

mean reported in table 5-1. The difference between the mean and the median provides further evidence of the right-skewed nature of the marginal damage distributions. Figure 5-4 indicates that damages are both more widespread and larger in magnitude when compared to figure 5-3. Again the impact of prevailing wind direction is evident; damages due to emissions from the facility in Indiana extend farthest from the source toward the northeast and southeast—a result of prevailing winds from the west. Figure 5-5 maps the impacts that correspond to the 95th percentile realization. The marginal damage in this case amounts to $25,290/ton

FIGURE 5-4

SPATIAL IMPACT OF SO_2 EMISSION FROM POWER PLANT IN INDIANA:
MEDIAN DRAW

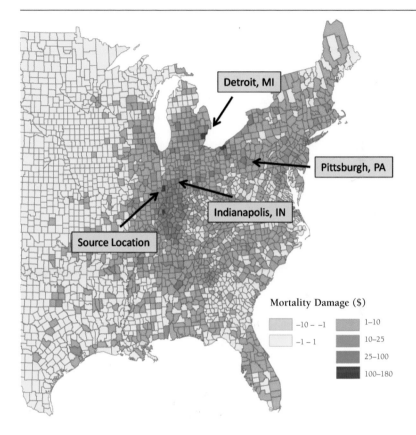

SO₂. This is more than two times larger than the mean value reported in table 5-1. In this outlier case, the impacts from the ton of SO_2 are evident over nearly the entire eastern half of the United States.

These figures indicate that as the percentile realization from the distribution increases, the level of damages increases because the impacts cover a larger and larger territory. In the 5th percentile case, the impact of an emission is largely local, with impacts primarily in the Midwest. One can be 95 percent certain that damages are larger than this. In the 95th percentile case, one can be 95 percent certain that damages are less than this. As one

FIGURE 5-5

SPATIAL IMPACT OF SO₂ EMISSION FROM POWER PLANT IN INDIANA:
95TH PERCENTILE DRAW

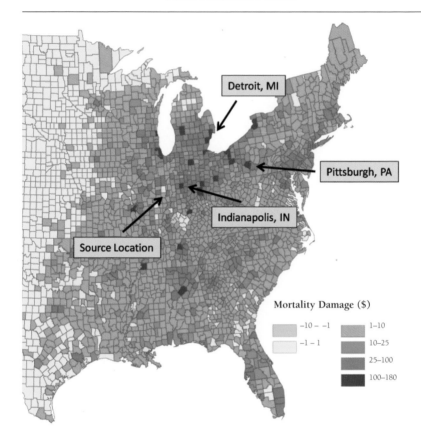

moves to the 50th and especially the 95th percentiles, the assumed range of damages is extended over an even larger territory; not only do midwestern cities endure large impacts, but so do southern and East Coast cities as well. The predicted set of receptor locations that are heavily impacted varies dramatically depending on whether the 5th percentile, the median, or the 95th percentile is used.

These findings have potentially important ramifications for policy. Figure 5-3, 5-4, and 5-5 show that over a wide range of damage estimates, impacts that are predicted to occur within the state that contains the power plant are relatively robust, as are impacts in cities within the same region. That is, regardless of whether the 5th or the 95th percentile impacts are used, the results suggest that damage will occur in midwestern states and cities therein. In contrast, impacts farther from the source are far less robust; the 95th percentile draw indicates large damages in cities on the East Coast, while the 5th percentile draw does not. These patterns clearly matter for policymakers who may use such damage estimates to assess the impacts of current or proposed facilities.

PART II

Policy Applications

6

A Case Study of Efficient Pollution Control: Sulfur Dioxide Emissions from Coal-fired Electric Power Generators

Chapter 1 demonstrated the desirability of efficient pollution-abatement policies using a theoretical model. However, the feasibility of such policies depends on the availability of marginal damage data in order to design efficient abatement strategies for specific sources of emissions. Regulators need to know firm-specific marginal damages if they are to implement efficient emission taxes or a cap-and-trade policy with optimal exchange rates. In this chapter, we explore how efficient policies to regulate SO_2 emissions could be developed for fossil fuel–fired power plants in the United States. We explore how SO_2 emissions would change as regulations move from the current uniform cap-and-trade program to a damage-differentiated efficient policy. The analysis involves two policy changes. In the first policy experiment, we introduce trading ratios described in chapter 1 that reflect the relative marginal damages of emissions for SO_2. In this experiment we assume that the aggregate cap in 2002 remains fixed: no change to aggregate emissions levels occurs. Rather, this case focuses on the manner in which the trading ratios lead to a reallocation of emissions relative to the observed distribution in 2002. In the second policy experiment, we alter the aggregate cap of emissions to equate expected marginal cost and expected marginal damage, as shown in chapter 1. The point of this simulation is to explore the spatial reallocation due to the trading ratios *conditional on* the optimal overall level of emissions. For both policy experiments, we compute the welfare improvement, the reduction in total social costs (which are defined as pollution damages plus abatement costs), and the distribution of emission changes across space.

In 1990 the U.S. Congress passed a set of amendments to the Clean Air Act that established a system of tradable permits—a cap-and-trade policy—governing SO_2 emissions produced by coal-fired electric power generators. Allowances, each valid for one ton of SO_2, were allocated to participants. In addition, the allowances could be banked for use in future years. Phase I of the cap-and-trade program took effect in 1995 and regulated approximately three hundred electric generating units. Phase II began in 2000 and regulated more than two thousand electric generating units. This cap-and-trade regime allows owners of permits to trade on a ton-for-ton basis. As explained in chapter 1, when faced with a uniform permit price, firms equate their marginal abatement costs to one another (by equating their marginal costs to the market price for permits). This distribution of emissions across regulated sources is cost-effective; it achieves aggregate abatement at the minimum total costs (Montgomery 1972).

In chapter 4 we demonstrated that the marginal damages of SO_2 vary by source location. This implies that the cost-effective allocation due to this uniform cap-and-trade program is not efficient. Because efficiency requires equating marginal damages to marginal abatement costs at each regulated source, if marginal damages are not equal for every polluter, then marginal costs should not be equal across polluting firms either. And, faced with one price for permits, firms seeking to minimize abatement costs tend to equate their marginal costs to the permit price and, hence, to one another. In the context of SO_2, this cannot be efficient.

As one can see in figure 6-1, regional differences exist; the marginal damages in the northern Midwest and Northeast are much greater than the marginal damages in the Rocky Mountains, Great Plains, and Southeast. Damages are also much higher near metropolitan centers. The high marginal damage especially in cities implies that, at the optimum allocation of emissions, sources in these locations should also have high marginal costs of abatement. Society should control emissions in cities more strictly than emissions in rural areas because they are more harmful on a ton-for-ton basis. A trading regime that induces firms to equate marginal costs to one another encourages too many emissions in high-damage locations and likely too few from rural, low-damage locations. Although marginal damages do not enter into the design of the original SO_2 trading program, they are integral to the efficient regulatory program explored in this chapter.

FIGURE 6-1
MARGINAL DAMAGE FOR ELECTRIC POWER GENERATORS IN TITLE IV
CAP-AND-TRADE PROGRAM AS OF 2002 ($/TON)

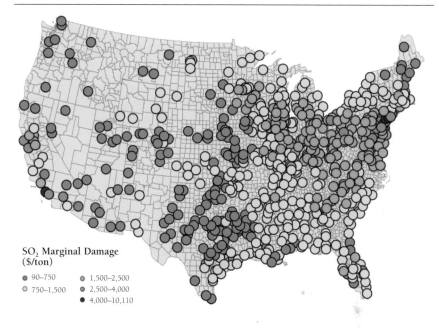

SO₂ Marginal Damage
($/ton)

- 90–750   ◑ 1,500–2,500
- ○ 750–1,500   ● 2,500–4,000
- ● 4,000–10,110

Methods

In keeping with the other analyses conducted herein, we examine the year 2002, during Phase II of the cap-and-trade program established by the 1990 amendments to the Clean Air Act (USEPA 2007). We examine two separate policy scenarios and the resulting welfare changes. The first step holds the observed aggregate emission target of 10.2 million tons of emissions constant and simply reallocates permits based on relative damages through the use of the trading ratios developed in chapter 1. This is equivalent to introducing a fixed exchange rate between sources equal to the inverse ratio of marginal damages. This comparison measures the welfare change of moving from uniform to differentiated permits. In the second case, we then estimate the welfare gain of moving to the efficient aggregate emission target that equates expected marginal damage to expected marginal cost. The model suggests that marginal damages exceed marginal costs, so the efficient aggregate target should be much smaller (between 1 and 2 million tons) depending on the form of the marginal cost function.

Functional forms for the marginal abatement cost and marginal damage function are used that fit the data. For the marginal abatement cost function, the observed abatement cost data for the power plants in the SO_2 program is from Keohane (2006). A constant elasticity form is fit to this data:

$$\frac{\partial C_i}{\partial X_i} = (\alpha + \delta_i)X_i^{\beta} \tag{6.1}$$

where: X_i = emissions from source (i)
C_i = abatement cost
α, β, δ_i = statistically estimated parameters

In this formulation, we assume that all firms face the same parameter (β) (which is the reciprocal of the price elasticity of abatement) and the same base intercept parameter (α). But each firm also has a firm-specific shift parameter (δ_i) that allows for heterogeneity in the level of marginal costs across firms. Heterogeneity in firms' marginal costs may be due to differences in abatement technology employed by firms, age of the plant, or firm-specific opportunities for substituting inputs in production (such as access to cleaner or more polluted fuel sources). We assume that $E[\delta] = 0$ and $E[\delta^2] = \sigma_c$.

The first step involves the derivation of the elasticity, or shape, parameter (β). We employ three different values of (β): -0.25, -0.50, and -1.00. As a point of reference, the elasticity reported in Carlson et al. (2000) that focused on SO_2 abatement costs is -0.34. In both policy scenarios, we test the sensitivity of firms' responses to the trading ratios to the different values of (β).[1]

The next step is to identify ($\alpha + \delta_i$), the source-specific intercept term in equation (6.1) for each electric generating unit. In order to estimate the *level* of marginal abatement costs for each firm, we rely on the fact that each electric generating unit in this analysis was regulated under the SO_2

---

1. The marginal costs in equation (6.1) are expressed as a function of the quantity of emissions $\beta = -0.25$, which implies an elasticity of emissions with respect to marginal costs of -4.

permit trading program in 2002. As a result, each firm faced a permit price of approximately \$175, the annual average permit price for 2002 (USEPA 2007). By assuming that the regulated firms chose to minimize their costs by equating their marginal abatement costs to the permit price, the marginal cost of each firm is equal to approximately \$175 in 2002, the market price of permits.[2] We then can solve for $(\alpha + \delta_i)$ using the following formula:

$$\alpha + \delta_i = \frac{175}{X_i^\beta} \tag{6.2}$$

In order to estimate the form of the marginal damage function, we conduct a number of experiments with the APEEP model. First we test whether the marginal damage of SO_2 emissions varies over a wide range of emissions produced by an individual source: from 0 to 15,000 tons. From these simulated marginal damages, we estimate a constant elasticity marginal damage function of the following form:

$$\frac{\partial D_i}{\partial X_i} = (\mu + \phi_i)X^\eta \tag{6.3}$$

where: X_i = emissions from source (i)
D_i = damage from emissions at source (i)
μ, η, ϕ_i = statistically estimated parameters

We find that $\eta = 0.000015$. This small value for the elasticity parameter suggests that the functional form of the marginal damage function for an individual power plant is effectively flat (see figure 6-2). The marginal damage is unresponsive to the firm's level of emissions. This is because the additional exposure to each receptor from even this wide range of emissions from a single source is quite small. The dose-response function and the valuation function are effectively linear for such small changes in exposure. It is important to note, however, that this design isolates the marginal damage function for individual sources by holding emissions from all sources

---

2. Although this assumption may not hold in practice for all sources, it is likely to approximate the cost level faced by many individual sources in the market.

FIGURE 6-2

MARGINAL DAMAGE FUNCTION FOR SO₂ EMISSIONS AT TWO POWER PLANTS

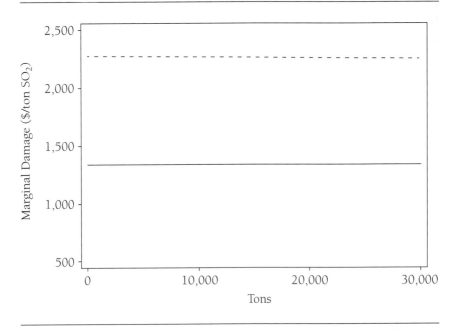

NOTE: Solid line = Colbert (Alabama) power plant emission, dash = Delmarva power plant (Delaware).

fixed while estimating the marginal damage function at a specific source. If emissions were to change at many facilities concurrently, we might observe some curvature in the marginal damage function.

Figure 6-2 reinforces the importance of location for two power plants. Figure 6-2 focuses on a large coal-fired power plant in rural Alabama and a large power plant in Delaware that is upwind from several major metropolitan areas. In comparing the marginal damage for SO₂ produced by the two power plants, we see that over a large range of emissions, the impact per ton is greater at the plant in Delaware. This is driven by human exposures per ton; the Delaware plant is upwind from many more people than the Alabama plant. As such, the marginal damage is greater for the Delaware plant. Hence, source location is a primary driver in determining marginal damages. It is also important to note that figure 6-2 shows the finding of a flat marginal damage function is robust across locations.

TABLE 6-1
WELFARE CHANGE FROM USING TRADING RATIOS THAT REFLECT MARGINAL
DAMAGE FOR DIFFERENT COST FUNCTIONS ($MILLION/YEAR)

Welfare Category	Marginal Abatement Cost Parameter		
	−4	−2	−1
Δ Abatement Costs	+856	+388	+154
Δ Pollution Damage	−1,954	−731	−285
Δ Social Cost	−1,098	−343	−131

NOTES: The aggregate cap on SO_2 remains fixed at 10 million tons. Social cost = pollution damages + abatement costs.

As a result of the finding that the marginal damage functions tend to be nearly perfectly flat, we simplify the marginal damage function in the following manner:

$$\frac{\partial D_i}{\partial X_i} = \mu + \phi_i \tag{6.4}$$

The marginal damage parameters ($\mu + \phi_i$) are estimated for each source using APEEP as described in chapter 4. In this analysis, we employ the deterministic marginal damage estimates that are reported in chapter 4.

Results

The welfare advantage due to employing the source-specific trading ratios is the reduction in the sum of total abatement costs and pollution damages across the entire sample of power plants in the analysis. Table 6-1 reports the results of these simulations in which the aggregate emission level is held fixed. The differentiated trading regime increases abatement costs but decreases pollution damages. Because the reduction in pollution damages is larger than the increase in abatement costs, the program increases social welfare.

The annual welfare improvement from introducing trading ratios into the SO_2 permit trading program ranges between $131 million and $1.1 billion, depending on the elasticity of the marginal cost of abatement.

FIGURE 6-3

CHANGE IN SO$_2$ EMISSIONS FROM TRADING RATIOS
WHEN THE MARGINAL COST ELASTICITY EQUALS −4

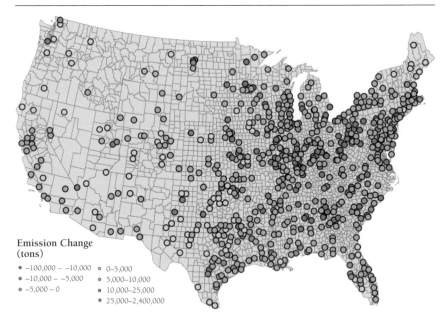

Emission Change
(tons)

- −100,000 – −10,000   ○ 0–5,000
- −10,000 – −5,000   ○ 5,000–10,000
- −5,000 – 0   ○ 10,000–25,000
  ○ 25,000–2,400,000

The more elastic the cost function (β = −0.25), the larger the increase in abatement costs, the larger the change in emissions, and the larger the welfare gain, *ceteris paribus*. Sources with relatively higher marginal damages must spend more on abatement, and low-damage sources spend less, relative to extant policy. The results in table 6-1 indicate that overall abatement costs increase; this implies that the abatement cost increase in high marginal damage sites is larger than the abatement cost reduction in low marginal damage sites. Despite this net increase in abatement costs, the program yields an overall welfare gain because the reduction in total damages is larger than the increase in abatement costs. The trading ratios make the abatement program far more effective at mitigating damages because it prioritizes reallocating the most harmful emissions to lower damage sites. However, if the marginal cost function is less elastic, there will be only a small response to changes in the price of SO$_2$ and thus little change in emissions.

FIGURE 6-4

CHANGE IN SO$_2$ EMISSIONS FROM TRADING RATIOS
WHEN THE MARGINAL COST ELASTICITY EQUALS –2

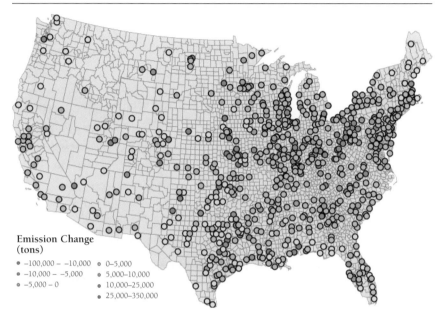

Emission Change
(tons)

- –100,000 – –10,000   ○ 0–5,000
- –10,000 – –5,000   ● 5,000–10,000
- –5,000 – 0   ● 10,000–25,000
  ● 25,000–350,000

Figure 6-3 shows how the change in emissions is allocated across plants when using β = –0.25 (marginal cost elasticity is equal to –4). The greatest decreases in emissions are concentrated in the Ohio River valley, the cities around the Great Lakes, and areas just upwind from the large eastern cities. These power plants correspond closely to the plants shown in figure 6-1 that have large marginal damages for SO$_2$. In low-damage locations, however, emissions increase. Most of the plants that would increase their emissions are located in the Pacific Northwest, Rocky Mountains, Great Plains, and northern New England. Figures 6-4 and 6-5 show the change in emissions that is projected to occur when the marginal cost elasticity is equal to –2 and –1, respectively. These figures indicate that the spatial pattern in the reallocation of emissions is quite robust to the different assumptions on the marginal cost function. The figures also emphasize the essence of the exchange rate policy; emissions are reallocated from high-damage to low-damage source locations based

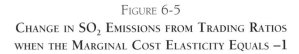

FIGURE 6-5
CHANGE IN SO$_2$ EMISSIONS FROM TRADING RATIOS
WHEN THE MARGINAL COST ELASTICITY EQUALS −1

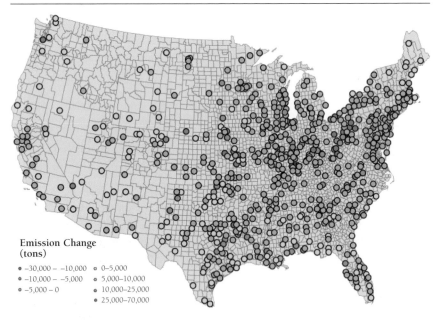

Emission Change (tons)

- −30,000 – −10,000   ○ 0–5,000
- −10,000 – −5,000   ● 5,000–10,000
- ○ −5,000 – 0   ● 10,000–25,000
- ● 25,000–70,000

on the difference in the relative harm of emissions. Trades are based on value rather than tonnage.

We now calculate the additional welfare gain of both changing the aggregate cap *and* reallocating emissions using the trading ratios. In this case, we move from the aggregate cap of 10.2 million tons of SO$_2$ mandated by the 1990 amendments to the Clean Air Act to the aggregate cap that equates marginal cost to marginal damage. We find that the efficient aggregate cap for SO$_2$ is roughly 1 million tons, but this value depends on the form of the marginal cost function. This suggests that even with the mandated reductions in allowances by 2010 to 8.95 million tons, the SO$_2$ trading regulations are far too lenient. Table 6-2 shows the change in abatement costs and damages in each scenario: net welfare increases from $8 billion to $11 billion. The range, as in table 6-1, depends on the form of the marginal cost function. In this example, the welfare improvement from this dramatic reduction in emissions overwhelms the improvement from using trading

TABLE 6-2

WELFARE CHANGE FROM USING TRADING RATIOS AND CHANGING AGGREGATE
EMISSION LEVELS TO OPTIMAL LEVEL ($MILLION/YEAR)

Welfare Category	Marginal Abatement Cost Elasticity		
	−4	−2	−1
Δ Abatement Costs	+2,356	+3,013	+3,485
Δ Pollution Damage	−13,400	−13,140	−11,633
Δ Social Cost	−11,044	−10,127	−8,148
Δ Emissions (million tons)	−10.15	−9.87	−8.61

NOTES: Aggregate cap on SO_2 as determined by marginal damage and marginal cost. The aggregate change in emissions is shown in bottom row. Social costs = pollution damages + abatement costs.

ratios. That is, in this case getting the aggregate cap right outweighs getting the relative prices right through the trading ratios. This result is peculiar to this example in the sense that the heterogeneity in damages across power plants is relatively small, while the degree to which the aggregate emission cap is set incorrectly is large.

To gain some perspective regarding the importance of moving regulations from a cost-effective cap-and-trade program to an efficient policy, we compare the magnitude of these welfare gains to the benefits of moving from command and control to the current cost-effective program for these power plants. Previous authors have estimated that the annual cost savings of the original SO_2 cap-and-trade program were between $150 million and $410 million (Schmalensee et al. 1998; Keohane 2006). The additional welfare gains of moving from uniform-price tradable permits to an efficient system of differentiated permits and efficient caps are ten times greater than the reduced abatement costs of cap and trade alone. These additional gains are likely to be worth the administrative and bureaucratic effort to improve the system. It is, however, important to note that in our policy experiments, generators do not face explicit constraints in term of demand for power. This is likely to attenuate the movement of emissions spatially and perhaps the projected welfare gains.

7

Setting Regulatory Priorities
Using Net Marginal Damages

In the previous chapter, we examined an efficient pollution policy for sulfur dioxide emissions from fossil fuel–fired electrical power plants. Although the theory of how to regulate pollution efficiently has been developed (Baumol and Oates 1988), policymakers have yet to adopt this approach. As described in chapter 1, air pollution policy in the United States is largely based on a command-and-control system through the use of performance standards, technology standards, and ambient standards. These policies do not have economic efficiency as their objective; they do not equate marginal cost to marginal damage. This chapter points out that many of these policies suffer from additional shortcomings. Specifically, they fail to regulate some source groups and categories, and they fail to regulate some pollutants. Although there are likely other deficiencies in current air pollution regulations, the failure to bring all pollutants and pollution sources under the regulatory scope is particularly problematic from an efficiency standpoint. Initial units of abatement are frequently both very cheap and very beneficial. Therefore, expanding the scope of regulations may yield considerable improvements to public health and environmental quality at a relatively lower cost than tightening existing regulations. This logic motivates the discussion of regulatory reform that follows.

An important constraint on the proposed transition to more efficient regulations made throughout this book centers on the costs associated with such a change; moving from a large, complex set of inefficient policies to a (perhaps more complex) set of perfectly efficient regulations will be costly. Regulators may have to follow elaborate processes involving appropriately considerable degrees of scientific and political scrutiny before making changes. There may also be high administrative costs to making changes in terms of retraining staff and promulgating new rules. Because it is not real-istic to reform all regulations at once, this chapter asks the following ques-tion: How should a regulatory agency determine which regulations are the highest priority to reform? We argue that an analysis of marginal damages and marginal costs can be used to prioritize regulatory reform as a second-best alternative to a more rapid transformation of current to efficient policy.

To prioritize regulatory reform based on a comparison of marginal dam-ages and marginal costs, we explore two simple political economy models of the administrative costs associated with a change in regulations. The first model assumes that administrative costs are a function of the change in emissions. In this context, the administrative costs of change are propor-tional to the number of regulated tons that must change. Policy changes that require greater emission adjustments impose greater administrative costs. The second model assumes that costs are driven by the number of sources affected. This implies that each regulated firm or consumer provides resis-tance to changes. Policy changes that affect a larger number of individual sources impose greater administrative costs.

If administrative costs are proportional to the change in the number of tons of emissions, regulators should focus on reforming the management of tons that are the most inefficiently regulated. This effort implies the need for policymakers to measure or determine degrees of inefficiency. A useful metric of the inefficiency of the rules (or lack thereof) that govern different sources and pollutants is the net marginal damage (NMD): the marginal damage of emissions minus the marginal cost of abatement.

Because regulations are efficient when marginal damages are equated to marginal abatement costs, emissions with the highest absolute value of NMD (either positive or negative) are the most inefficient. Society stands to gain the most, in a welfare sense, from changing the emission levels of sources with large (absolute value) NMD. For instance, if NMD is very large and positive, it implies that the marginal damage far exceeds the marginal cost of abatement and that there is an important opportunity to abate more. Symmetrically, if the NMD is very large and negative, it implies that marginal cost far exceeds marginal damage and that society has over-regulated this emission. This rule requires identifying which specific tons are regulated most inefficiently (the widest gap between marginal damage and marginal cost) and targeting these tons for reform. We are suggesting a regulatory reform initiative that should give these high NMD tons the highest priority. Hence, if administrative costs are driven by the number of tons affected, this approach maximizes society's return per ton of reform.

In order to implement this NMD approach, regulators need to have information on both marginal damages and marginal costs by source and pollutant. Chapter 4 provides the marginal damages due to emissions for each source in the United States. Information about the current marginal cost of abatement for some source types is available from the U.S. Environmental Agency (USEPA 1999). Specifically, we estimate the average per-ton abatement costs from the cost data reported by USEPA (1999). We intend this approach to be a demonstration of how using the NMD to reform current policies would work. In order to undertake this process in practice, we would need more detailed cost modeling to form the basis of the marginal cost estimates. In addition, because of data constraints, in this chapter we assume that unregulated sources and/or pollutants have initial costs per ton equal to zero. However, if the actual marginal abatement costs schedules have a large vertical intercept, then our assumption will yield overestimates of the NMD. Using these data combined with the marginal damage data reported in chapter 4, we demonstrate the methodology proposed above by computing the NMD for several source categories.

These source categories, which are used in the USEPA's emission inventories, include utilities, nonutility point sources, commercial area sources, residences, farms, and a collection of mobile sources differentiated by vehicle type, fuel type, and on-road versus off-road usage (USEPA 1999). We estimate separate NMDs for urban and rural sources because the marginal damages differ by such a large margin according to this land use distinction. Each source type is then placed into one of three priority categories based on its current NMD.

We also tabulate the total damage caused by emissions from each source group. We undertake this additional task because, if certain regulatory reforms have a high fixed cost, the regulatory agency should also focus on the magnitude of damages as well per source type. That is, it may not be socially beneficial to make the reform if there are high administrative costs to making particular changes in the regulations. The agency would want to be sure that the magnitude of the overall gains is worth making the change. Therefore, in addition to estimating NMD, the regulator should also calculate the gross external damages from each source. GED, as noted in the introduction and described in more detail in chapter 8, is a measure of the total damages caused by a particular source. It is defined as the marginal damages times the tons of emissions by that source. Below we calculate the total damages that are caused by emissions from each source category. This identifies what fraction of the GED from air pollution is produced by sources in each of the four priority categories.

Analytical Model

As was shown in chapter 1, the efficient rule for the environmental regulator is to minimize the social costs from controlling emissions (X_i) from source (i):

$$\min_{X_i} \sum_{i=1}^{N} C_i(X_i) + \sum_{i=1}^{N} D_i(X_i) \tag{7.1}$$

And as in chapter 4, the efficient outcome equates marginal damage to marginal cost for all sources:

$$\left(\frac{\partial D_i}{\partial X_i}\right) = -\left(\frac{\partial C_i}{\partial X_i}\right) \nabla_i \tag{7.2}$$

If, through the use of inefficient designs, existing policies lead to inefficient rules, then (7.2) will not be satisfied. This will lead to two possible outcomes. Marginal damage will exceed marginal cost, suggesting that regulations be tightened, or marginal cost will exceed marginal damage, suggesting regulations be loosened. The bigger the difference is between marginal cost and marginal damage, the more important is the regulatory reform.

Figure 7-1 employs a simple example, the case of two industries, to display the argument graphically. The two industries have different marginal cost and marginal damage functions, labeled MC_1 and MD_1 for industry (1) and MC_2 and MD_2 for industry (2). If regulations forced them to have the same emissions, for instance an emission limit of X, firms in industry (1) would pollute at nearly the efficient level, where MC_1 is approximately equal to MD_1. For industry (1), the net marginal damage $MC_1 - MD_1$ is shown as the dashed line from b to c. Note that NMD_1 is relatively small. However, at the same level of emissions (X), the level of emissions for

FIGURE 7-1

NET MARGINAL DAMAGE FOR TWO INDUSTRIES

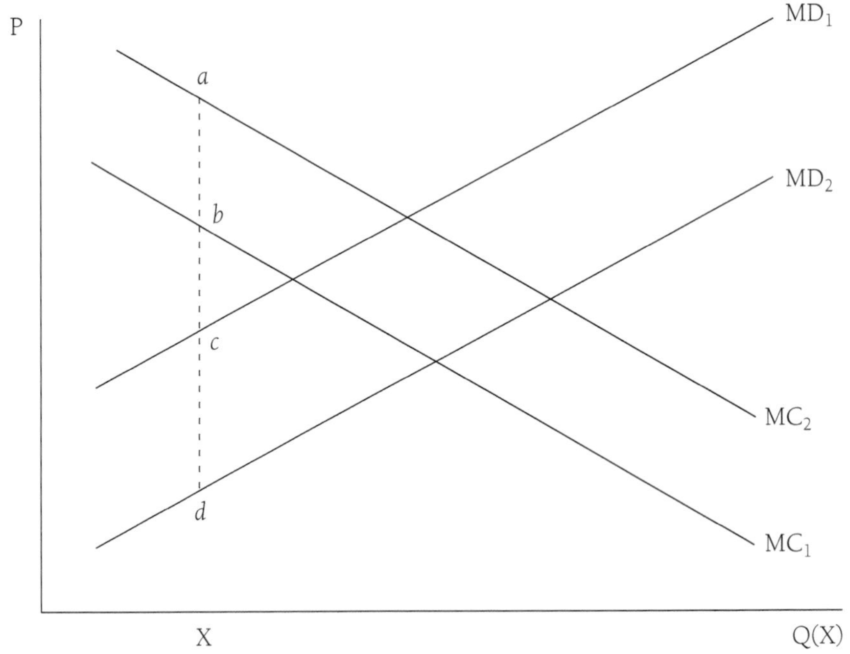

industry (2) is considerably lower than the efficient choice for this industry where $MC_2 = MD_2$. As a result, the inefficiency for industry (2) is significantly greater; NMD_2 (shown as the distance a − d in figure 7-1) is much larger. The prescription for regulatory reform would place a higher priority on adjusting the emission level of industry (2) than industry (1).

In order to connect this point back to the variation in marginal damages reported in chapter 4, in figure 7-2 we show the importance of differences in NMD for two industries with identical costs of abatement. In this case, the only difference between the two firms is the level of the marginal damage functions. Note that this particular scenario is likely to occur if two firms in the same industry are located in an urban and a rural area. In this case NMD_1 is represented by the distance b − c, and NMD_2 is given by a − d.

FIGURE 7-2

NET MARGINAL DAMAGE FOR TWO INDUSTRIES
WITH IDENTICAL ABATEMENT TECHNOLOGY

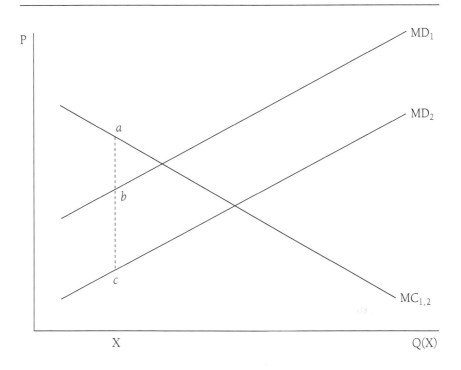

Even with identical abatement technology, the NMD differs significantly, and the prescription for regulatory reform using NMD would place a higher priority on adjusting the emission level of industry (2) than industry (1).

Results

Because regulators would require information about marginal damage to implement this approach to regulatory reform, table 7-1 reports average marginal damages by pollutant and source location for point and area sources. Urban emissions are generally more dangerous than rural emissions because they lead to more human exposures per ton, and human

TABLE 7-1
MARGINAL DAMAGE BY SOURCE TYPE AND POLLUTANT ($/TON/YEAR)

Source Type	$PM_{2.5}$	PM_{10}	NO_x	SO_2	VOCs	NH_3
Area Urban	9,080	810	490	3,300	960	10,920
Point Urban	4,850	470	340	2,230	530	5,710
Area Rural	2,640	220	460	1,600	290	2,250
Point Rural	1,970	190	400	1,430	230	1,710

health effects constitute the largest share of damages (see chapter 8). In urban areas, area sources have higher marginal damages than point sources because area sources tend to discharge emissions at ground level whereas point sources tend to have high stacks. In urban areas, ground-level emissions lead to higher damages because they increase local concentrations, which then lead to high human exposures. In contrast, emissions from tall smokestacks are dispersed and take a long time to come to ground, leading to much lower local concentrations and therefore much lower exposures when emitted in cities. Smokestacks are very effective at diminishing local exposures. Therefore, ground-level emissions cause much higher damages than smokestack emissions when both are released in cities. But the difference between ground-level and smokestack marginal damages is much smaller in rural areas. This pattern of differences in the impact of emission based on release height is evident in table 7-1. For $PM_{2.5}$, urban emissions released at the ground level (area sources) are nearly two times more harmful than emissions from smokestacks (point sources). But rural emissions released at ground level are only one-third more harmful than emissions released from smokestacks. Similarly, urban discharges of PM_{10}, VOCs, and NH_3 are also roughly twice as dangerous when generated at the ground as opposed to being released from a point source. The difference between ground and smokestack emissions is much smaller for rural emissions. The principle remains true for SO_2 and NO_x, but the difference is smaller for these two pollutants because they take longer to form harmful secondary pollutants.

As was reported in chapter 4, table 7-1 shows considerable variability in the marginal damage of emissions across pollutants. Table 7-1 also shows that there is considerable heterogeneity in marginal damages by

TABLE 7-2
AVERAGE ABATEMENT COST BY SOURCE TYPE AND POLLUTANT ($/TON/YEAR)

Source Type	$PM_{2.5}$	PM_{10}	NO_x	SO_2	VOCs	NH_3
Agriculture	2,500	2,500	0	0	0	0
Commercial Nonpoint	0	0	1,300	0	300	0
Residential	0	0	0	0	0	0
Fugitive Dust	2,500	2,500	0	0	0	0
On-Road Mobile	2,000	2,000	1,100	2,000	700	0
Off-Road Mobile	0	0	500	0	100	0
Utility	0	0	500	300	0	0
Non-Utility Point	0	0	1,900	0	800	0

source location and release height. Regulations that tend to treat all firms as if their emissions are equally harmful will consequently lead to a wide range of NMD values.

Table 7-2 displays average abatement cost estimates by source (USEPA 1999). Zero marginal cost estimates imply the source types and pollutants that are unregulated at the federal level. As discussed above, the marginal costs associated with initial levels of abatement for these unregulated sources may not be zero, but it is likely that the initial marginal costs are low. Note that even for the regulated sources (those with abatement costs greater than zero), there is a great deal of variation in the average cost per ton across sources for the same pollutant (except particulates). For example, the average cost of abatement of VOCs from off-road mobile (vehicles) is $100/ton, but for on-road mobile (vehicles) it is $700/ton. This is because there are more stringent regulations for on-road vehicles. Furthermore, SO_2 abatement is relatively inexpensive for utilities compared to on-road mobile. Finally, abatement of NO_x from utilities and off-road mobile is less expensive than abatement from nonutility point sources and commercial nonpoint sources.

In table 7-3, we combine the information about marginal damages and marginal costs to determine the priority of controlling individual types of sources and pollutants. This ranking uses the NMD approach discussed above. Specifically, the ranking is made based on the difference between marginal damages and marginal abatement costs: the NMD. Sources with

TABLE 7-3
REGULATORY PRIORITY USING NET BENEFIT PER TON BY SOURCE TYPES

Source Location, Type	$PM_{2.5}$	PM_{10}	NO_x	SO_2	NH_3	VOC
Urban						
Stationary Agriculture	H	L	M	H	H	M
Commercial Area	H	M	L	H	H	M
Residential Fuel Combustion	H	M	M	H	H	M
Utility	H	L	L	H	H	M
Non-Utility Point	H	L	L	H	H	L
Mobile Nonroad and Heavy-Duty Gas	H	M	L	H	H	M
Off-Road Diesels	H	M	L	H	H	M
Light-Duty Gas Cars and Trucks	H	L	L	H	H	L
Highway Diesels	H	L	L	H	H	L
Rural						
Stationary Agriculture	L	L	L	H	H	L
Commercial Area	H	L	L	H	H	L
Residential Fuel Combustion	H	L	L	H	H	L
Utility	H	L	L	H	H	L
Non-Utility Point	H	L	L	H	H	L
Mobile Nonroad and Heavy-Duty Gas	H	L	L	H	H	L
Off-Road Diesels	H	L	L	H	H	L
Light-Duty Gas Cars and Trucks	M	L	L	L	H	L
Highway Diesels	M	L	L	L	H	L

NOTE: H = high priority for more abatement (NMD > \$1,000), M = medium priority for more abatement (NMD \$500–\$1,000), and L = low priority for change in abatement (NMD < \$500).

higher NMD should be assigned a higher priority for reform by the regulator. The categorization scheme in table 7-3 divides sources by urban and rural location, by types of stationary sources (such as agriculture and commercial sites), and by different types of mobile sources (such as vehicles, marine vessels, and aircraft). A high priority for future abatement is given to sources with NMD greater than \$1,000/ton, a medium priority is given to sources with NMD between \$500/ton and \$1,000/ton, and a low priority is assigned to sources with NMD less than \$500. The low-priority category includes some sources with negative NMD (marginal abatement costs exceed marginal damages of emissions). We could not identify any sources with large negative NMD except possibly ground-level controls of NO_x in urban areas.

In urban areas, all stationary emissions of SO_2, NH_3, and $PM_{2.5}$ are in the high-priority group. This list reflects the emissions and sources with marginal damages that are much higher than their marginal cost of abatement.

The urban sources in the lowest-priority category are PM_{10} emitted from all point and agricultural sources as well as on-road vehicles. PM_{10} emissions from commercial area sources, residential combustion of fuels, and both types of off-road vehicles are placed in the medium-priority group. Emissions of NO_x from all source categories except residential fuel combustion and agriculture fall into the low-priority group. These latter two sources of NO_x fit into the medium-priority class. VOC generated by agricultural sources, commercial area sources, residential fuel combustion, utilities, and both types of off-road vehicles fit into the medium-priority group. The remaining sources of VOC fall into the low-priority class. Some of the "low-priority" sources simply have low marginal damages. However, other "low-priority" sources are already nearly efficiently regulated (their marginal damages are already very close to marginal costs), so there is little potential gain from changing their standards or regulations. The marginal damages from the middle-priority sources exceed the marginal cost of abatement by a considerable margin, so there is room to improve the efficiency of these regulations. The potential gain per ton is lower than with the high-priority sources, but there are some sources in this category that involve a lot of damage. For example, there is a substantial amount of urban PM_{10} emissions from area and mobile sources.

In rural areas, the only emissions in the high-priority category are SO_2, $PM_{2.5}$, and NH_3. Among emissions of these three pollutants, only $PM_{2.5}$ emissions from agriculture (low), light-duty cars and trucks, and highway diesel sources (both medium), as well as SO_2 emissions from highway diesels and light-duty cars and trucks (low), do not fall into the high-priority bin. In rural areas, all emissions of PM_{10} and VOCs are a low priority for abatement. This also holds for all sources of NO_x.

Tightening regulations on sources with high net marginal damages, however, does not necessarily identify sources of large amounts of GED. If each source is difficult to regulate, that is, if it is costly to transition current policies to encompass these additional sources, the regulator may

TABLE 7-4

PERCENTAGE SHARE GED (PERCENTAGE SHARE TONNAGE)

Regulatory Priority	Urban	Rural	Total
High	48 (12)	19 (15)	67 (27)
Medium	12 (7)	1 (4)	13 (11)
Low	11 (28)	9 (34)	20 (62)

want to focus on only sources with large amounts of GED *and* high net marginal damages.

Table 7-4 displays the fraction of GED and the fraction of national tonnage generated by sources in each priority classification for urban and rural sources. Emissions from high-priority sources are responsible for 67 percent of the GED. However, high-priority sources generate only 27 percent of emissions by weight. One critical key to regulatory reform is to pay more attention to the harm caused by emissions from each source type and less to the tonnage produced by each source type. Although these high-priority emissions do not involve much tonnage, their elimination will do a lot to reduce air pollution damages. Table 7-4 also reveals that over 70 percent of the high-priority damages are generated by sources in urban areas. By focusing on urban high-priority targets, regulators can eliminate almost half of the damages from air pollution in the United States. So the focus on high NMD urban emissions is justified both in terms of the difference between marginal damage and marginal cost and their high total GED.

The medium-priority sources generate 13 percent of the GED. Urban emissions dominate this group, accounting for almost 90 percent of the damages. The medium category contributes 11 percent of the tonnage. Taken together with high-priority emissions, these results suggest that 80 percent of the remaining damages from air pollution are in these top two categories.

In contrast, sources in the low-priority category, those yielding NMD less than $500/ton, produce 20 percent of the GED. The low-priority category accounts for 62 percent of total emissions by tonnage. One way to view this result is that the USEPA is already regulating almost two-thirds of emissions in a relatively efficient manner. That is, marginal damages and marginal costs are nearly equal. Unfortunately, the emissions in this

TABLE 7-5

PERCENTAGE SHARE GED (PERCENTAGE SHARE TONNAGE)

Regulatory Priority	$PM_{2.5}$	PM_{10}	NO_x	NH_3	SO_2	VOC	Total
High	24 (4)	0 (0)	0 (0)	14 (5)	28 (18)	0 (0)	67 (27)
Medium	1 (1)	3 (7)	0 (0)	0 (0)	0 (0)	10 (3)	13 (11)
Low	1 (1)	4 (17)	8 (26)	0 (0)	0 (0)	7 (18)	20 (62)
Total	26 (6)	7 (24)	8 (26)	14 (5)	28 (18)	17 (21)	100 (100)

low-priority category only account for one-fifth of all damages. The policy implication is that the regulations for low-priority emissions should be left as they are. Regulators should now prioritize increased abatement of the medium- and high-priority emissions. This would dramatically improve the overall efficiency of the Clean Air Act and increase society's return on its abatement investments.

Table 7-5 displays the fraction of GED and the fraction of national emissions in each priority classification by pollutant. High-priority emissions are caused almost entirely by emissions of $PM_{2.5}$, NH_3, and SO_2. High-priority $PM_{2.5}$ causes about 25 percent of GED and high-priority NH_3 causes 14 percent of the GED, even though they amount to just 4 percent and 5 percent of national emissions by tonnage, respectively. High-priority SO_2 emissions account for another 28 percent of GED and another 18 percent of national tonnage. PM_{10} and VOC account for almost all of the medium-ranked damage. Table 7-5 clearly highlights the importance of tightening controls on $PM_{2.5}$, NH_3, and SO_2.

Almost all of the emissions from low-priority sources are discharges of PM_{10}, NO_x, and VOC. Low-priority emissions of these three pollutants constitute 20 percent of the GED and 62 percent of total emissions. Regulations of these three pollutants are already close to being efficient, and so further reform of the regulations covering these pollutants is unlikely to yield large efficiency gains.

The findings in this chapter highlight the importance of using marginal damages, combined in this setting with estimates of marginal costs, to reformulate the current federal regulatory program for local air pollutants. The NMD methodology reveals that current regulations of the majority of VOC,

NO_x, and PM_{10} emissions are nearly efficient. The regulations that most need adjustment involve discharges of SO_2, $PM_{2.5}$, and NH_3. Many of these emissions are underregulated and need to be tightened. Specifically, urban emissions of SO_2, $PM_{2.5}$, and NH_3 need to be made more stringent. Tighter regulations of these specific emissions will reduce the gap between marginal cost and marginal damage. Increasing the stringency of regulations applied to these discharges would address emissions that produce nearly half of the damage from U.S. air pollution emissions. Careful adjustments of U.S. air pollution regulations based on NMD could dramatically improve efficiency.

PART III

Measurement of Air Pollution Damages

8

The Gross External Damages from Air Pollution in the United States

In this chapter we compute the gross external damages of air pollution for the six pollutants covered by the APEEP model. We employ the marginal damage associated with emitting an additional ton of pollution from nearly ten thousand sources in the United States computed by the APEEP model. The total damages produced by a source are equal to the marginal damage of an emission (i.e., its shadow price) times the total tons emitted from a specific source. Adding the total damages together across all sources yields the GED, which is a green accounting parallel to GDP (Nordhaus and Kokkelenberg 1999; Muller, Mendelsohn, and Nordhaus 2011). Both GED and GDP measure the value of production by computing the sum of the quantity of each good produced times its current price or marginal value. We also include the damage caused by carbon dioxide emissions.

Our analysis employs marginal values instead of average values to compute the GED for three primary reasons. First, by measuring marginal damages for each pollutant, we can explore policies that target emissions of each pollutant. As discussed in chapter 1, policymakers should use the marginal damages—not the average damages—to determine optimal regulations. Specifically, policymakers should set marginal damage equal to the marginal cost of abatement for each emission. Second, as reported in chapter 4, marginal damages of pollution vary substantially across space. Hence, applying spatially specific shadow prices will yield a more accurate assessment of total damage than relying on spatially averaged values. Third, using marginal damage to measure aggregate damage is consistent with national income accounts. Both measures are intended to compare changes in the aggregate, not all-or-nothing values. For example, GDP measures are used to see how much the economy is changing between time periods.

The GED is intended to track how the damage from pollution is chang-ing over time, just as GDP tracks changes in economic activity. The GED is also useful for comparing the size of pollution damage relative to the econ-omy. Policymakers need to know whether this damage is a trivial fraction of GDP or a very large fraction of it. This book only presents GED values for 2002. More research is needed to track how GED changes over time.

This chapter presents results for the entire U.S. economy. Chapters 9 and 10 decompose the GED by sectors of the economy and by industries, respectively. Together, these three chapters illustrate that it is possible to have a detailed measure of air pollution damages in the National Income and Product Accounts. This is an important step toward generating green accounts.

This chapter reports the GED using the approach to marginal damage measurement discussed in chapters 2, 3, and 4. This entails running the APEEP model for a baseline case and then invoking the marginal damage algorithm approximately sixty thousand times to cover all six pollutants and all ten thousand sources encompassed by APEEP. These source- and pollutant-specific marginal damages are then multiplied by the reported emissions generated by each source of each pollutant species as shown in equation 8.1.

$$GED_{s,j} = X_{s,j} \times MD_{s,j} \qquad (8.1)$$

where $X_{s,j}$ = annual emission of pollutant (s) generated by source (j),[1] and $MD_{s,j}$ = the per-ton damage produced by source (j) also for pollutant (s).

Table 8-1 reports the GED from 2002 emissions of air pollution in the United States. In the baseline scenario, GED is $109 billion, or 1.0 percent of 2002 GDP. Reductions in the quality of human health and longevity make up 97 percent of the total damages from air pollution. Premature mortalities constitute 83 percent, and illnesses constitute 14 percent of the total damages. Nonhealth impacts are relatively small, only 4 percent of the total damages. These consist of reduced agricultural yields ($0.8 billion),

---

1. In this and subsequent chapters we change our notation from (i) indexing firm or source to (j). This change occurs because in subsequent chapters, (i) references industry or sector rather than an individual source.

TABLE 8-1
GROSS EXTERNAL DAMAGE ($BILLION/YEAR)

Pollutant	Mortality	Morbidity	Agriculture	Timber	Visibility	Materials	Recreation	Total
PM$_{2.5}$	26.3	2.0	0	0	0.3	0	0	28.6
PM$_{10}$	0	6.2	0	0	1.0	0	0	7.2
NO$_x$	6.7	0.7	0.5	0.04	0.2	0	0.02	8.2
NH$_3$	14.0	1.5	0	0	0.2	0	0	15.7
SO$_2$	27.2	3.1	0	0	0.4	0.1	0	30.8
VOCs	15.8	1.8	0.2	0.02	0.2	0	0	18.0
Total	90.0	15.3	0.8	0.06	2.4	0.1	0.02	108.6[a]

a = Row and column totals may not be precisely equal because of rounding.

the present value of reduced timber yields ($60 million), visibility loss ($2.4 billion), accelerated depreciation of man-made materials ($100 million), and lost recreation usage due to impaired forest health ($20 million).

Table 8-1 also shows the relative contribution of each pollutant to total damages. (It is important to note that this refers to the share of damages caused by emissions of each type of pollutant, not the share of damages caused by ambient concentrations.) Emissions of the following four pollutants cause the greatest damage: PM$_{2.5}$, NH$_3$, SO$_2$, and VOCs. These four pollutants make up half of all emissions by weight, and yet they cause 85 percent of total damages.

Table 8-2 shows that PM$_{2.5}$ emissions produce 26 percent of total damages ($29 billion), although they are only 6 percent of total emissions by weight (4.7 million tons). PM$_{2.5}$ emissions are so harmful because they directly affect mortality rates when and where they are emitted. Most other pollutants must transform into PM$_{2.5}$ or ozone in order to affect mortality rates, and become dispersed before people are exposed to such emissions. Emissions of NH$_3$ are 5 percent of total emissions by weight (4 million tons) but cause 15 percent of total damages ($16 billion). All of the damages from NH$_3$ emissions stem from their role as a catalyst in the formation of PM$_{2.5}$ through interactions with NO$_x$ and SO$_2$. Emissions of SO$_2$ make up 19 percent of the total by weight (14.8 million tons), and they generate 28 percent of total damages ($30.8 billion). Most of the SO$_2$ damages are due to the formation of sulfate (an important component of PM$_{2.5}$). VOC emissions are

TABLE 8-2
GED AND EMISSION SHARES

Pollutant	% GED	% Emissions	% GED / % Emission
$PM_{2.5}$	26	6	4.4
PM_{10}	7	20	0.3
NO_x	7	28	0.3
NH_3	15	5	2.9
SO_2	28	19	1.5
VOC	17	22	0.8

22 percent of the total emissions (17 million tons) but cause 17 percent of total damages ($18 billion). VOC emissions contribute to the formation of both ozone and $PM_{2.5}$.

Table 8-2 also indicates that NO_x and PM_{10} account for almost half of the total tonnage but only 14 percent of damages. NO_x emissions are 28 percent of the total emissions (21 million tons) but cause only 7 percent of the GED ($8 billion in damages). These damages include the influence of NO_x emissions on both $PM_{2.5}$ and tropospheric ozone. Finally, PM_{10} emissions (which in APEEP are modeled as net of $PM_{2.5}$) account for 20 percent of total emissions (16 million tons) but only 7 percent of the GED (or $7 billion in damages).[2]

The third column of table 8-2 provides a measure of the relative contribution of each pollutant to total damages and total mass emitted. Pollutants that generate large damages with small quantities of emissions have a ratio of GED to emissions greater than one. These include $PM_{2.5}$, NH_3, and SO_2, with GED to emission ratios of 4.4, 2.9, and 1.5, respectively. Pollutants that cause smaller amounts of damage but that have copious amounts of emissions show a ratio that is less than one. These include PM_{10}, NO_x, and VOC, with GED to emission ratios of 0.3, 0.3, and 0.8, respectively.[3]

---

2. In these calculations, $PM_{2.5}$ emissions have been subtracted from PM_{10} emissions. Thus, PM_{10} includes all particles greater than 2.5 microns in diameter but less than 10 microns in diameter.

3. Note that the ratios are proportional; the percentage of total GED is divided by the percentage of total emissions.

TABLE 8-3
EMISSIONS, MARGINAL DAMAGES, AND GED
BY POLLUTANT AND SOURCE LOCATION

Source Location	$PM_{2.5}$	PM_{10}	NO_x	NH_3	SO_2	VOC	Total	(%)
Urban (million tons/year)	2.0	6.1	12.2	1.2	8.0	10.3	39.8	52
Rural (million tons/year)	2.7	9.4	8.8	2.8	6.8	6.3	36.8	48
Urban ($/ton)	6,070	570	380	7,210	2,540	650		
Rural ($/ton)	2,180	200	420	1,880	1,490	250		
Urban ($billion/year)	20.9	5.1	4.3	11.3	20.0	15.9	77.5	71
Rural ($billion/year)	7.7	2.1	3.9	4.5	10.9	2.2	31.2	29

NOTE: Urban emissions and marginal damages are positively correlated so that total damages are more than the product of the average urban damage per ton times the urban tons emitted.

Table 8-3 explores how the spatially detailed approach, modeling the damages per ton at specific source locations, captures differences in the effects of urban and rural emissions. Table 8-3 displays the average of source-specific marginal damages for each pollutant from all urban and all rural locations. The marginal damages from urban emissions are greater than the marginal damages from rural emissions for every pollutant except NO_x. For example, the marginal damages from NH_3 are nearly four times larger for urban versus rural sources, and the marginal damages from $PM_{2.5}$ emissions are three times larger for sources in cities than for sources in the country. The marginal damages for emissions of VOC, SO_2, and PM_{10} from urban areas are roughly two times larger than the marginal damages for rural emissions of these pollutants. However, there is almost no difference in the magnitude of the marginal damage for emissions of NO_x between urban and rural sources. NO_x emissions are not more harmful in cities because background levels of NO_x are often sufficiently high that additional emissions of NO_x reduce O_3 (Seinfeld and Pandis 1998). This titration effect reduces the marginal damage of urban emissions of NO_x.

Table 8-3 displays how emissions are distributed across rural and urban counties. There are about as many tons of emissions in both types of counties. Of course, the rural counties account for the vast majority of acreage in the contiguous states. Emissions per unit area are consequently much lower in rural counties on average. Concentrations of pollution therefore also tend to be lower in rural areas than in urban areas. Furthermore, the marginal damage of urban emissions tends to be higher because these emissions cause more human exposures per ton due to the higher population density. Consequently, although urban emissions are almost the same magnitude as rural emissions by weight, they cause 71 percent of total damages, and rural emissions cause only 29 percent. Large rural point sources are important in determining the spatial distribution of emissions and the GED because they emit such large amounts of emissions, and yet the bulk of air pollution damages comes from metropolitan emissions.

The urban emissions of every pollutant cause more damage than the rural emissions. Urban VOC emissions are responsible for 88 percent of VOC damage; urban $PM_{2.5}$, PM_{10}, and NH_3 emissions generate approximately 70 percent of the damage caused by these pollutants. For SO_2 and NO_x, 66 percent of the total damage is caused by urban emissions.

The aggregate values reported in table 8-1 are obtained by multiplying the marginal damage at each source times the emissions at that source. For $PM_{2.5}$ and VOC in particular, the aggregate damages from these pollutants are not equal to multiplying the average urban marginal damage (reported in table 8-3) times the tons of urban emissions. For example, multiplying the average urban marginal damage for $PM_{2.5}$ of \$6,070 by the quantity of emissions of 2 million tons yields total urban damages of \$12.1 billion. However, table 8-3 reports that the aggregate source-specific damage of urban $PM_{2.5}$ is \$20.9 billion. The positive correlation between the tonnage of emissions and marginal damage leads to this much higher value. The urban sources with the highest marginal damage also tend to have the largest quantities of emissions.

In contrast, there were 8 million tons of SO_2 emitted in urban areas in 2002. These are valued, on average at \$2,540 per ton. These values, coupled with the reported tonnage, suggest an urban GED for SO_2 of about \$20 billion. This is nearly identical to the urban GED for SO_2 that is computed using the source-specific marginal damages and emissions reported in table 8-3. Hence, there is no such correlation between emission quantities and marginal damages for SO_2.

All the aggregate values in the chapter to date refer just to emissions of NH_3, NO_x, $PM_{2.5}$, PM_{10}, SO_2, and VOC. For comparison, Table 8-4 reports the damage associated with emissions of CO_2. Approximately 5,880 million tons of CO_2 were emitted in the United States in 2002 (U.S. Energy

TABLE 8-4
GROSS EXTERNAL DAMAGES FROM CARBON DIOXIDE
EMITTED IN THE UNITED STATES

Pollutant	Emissions (million tons)	GED_l	GED_c	GED_h
Damage/ton		$4	$8	$29
Damages of CO_2	5,880	24×10^9	47×10^9	170×10^9

NOTE: The damage per ton reflects the present value of future damages (Tol 2005).

Information Administration 2008). The literature reports a range of damages per ton of CO_2. These damages reflect the present value of the stream of future damage caused by a ton of emissions today. We employ three alternative damage estimates reported by Tol (2005): a low estimate of $4, a central estimate of $8, and a high estimate of $29 per ton of CO_2. Note that for greenhouse gas emissions, the location of the emission does not affect the magnitude of damages. Employing the lower estimate for damage per ton of CO_2 produces a total GED of $133 billion ($24 billion due to CO_2), the central estimate produces a total GED of $156 billion ($47 billion due to CO_2), and the high estimate produces a GED of $279 billion ($170 billion due to CO_2). Relative to 2002 GDP, including CO_2 damages implies that the GED of air pollution plus CO_2 comprise 1.3, 1.5, and 2.6 percent of GDP for the lower, central, and high CO_2 damage estimates.

Table 8-5 duplicates the analysis shown in table 8-2 except that it includes CO_2. The results are striking. CO_2 emissions account for 99 percent of total emissions by weight but lead to only 30 percent of total damages (when using the central damage estimate of $8/ton). Each of the remaining pollutants contributes less than 1 percent of total emissions. And yet the share of GED for each of the six local pollutants is appreciable (greater than or equal to 5 percent). Looking at the ratio of the percent GED divided by the percent of emissions reveals that the ratio is 0.3 for CO_2 but is 13 or higher for all the other pollutants. Although there is a vast amount of CO_2 emitted in the United States per annum, local pollutants cause more harm than CO_2. Of course, as greenhouse gases (GHGs) accumulate in the atmosphere, the marginal damage of CO_2 will rise. Eventually, CO_2 will become more harmful than local pollutants. However, current research suggests that

TABLE 8-5
SHARE GED AND EMISSIONS INCLUDING CO_2

Pollutant	% GED (central)	% Emissions	% GED / % Emissions (low)	% GED / % Emissions (central)	% GED / % Emissions (high)
$PM_{2.5}$	18	0.0	216	183	102
PM_{10}	5	0.3	18	15	9
NO_x	5	0.4	15	13	7
NH_3	10	0.0	119	101	57
SO_2	20	0.2	78	66	37
VOCs	12	0.3	46	39	22
CO_2	30	99	0.1	0.3	0.6

the damage from CO_2 will probably not exceed the damage from local pollutants until after the middle of the twenty-first century (Nordhaus 2008).

In addition to the base scenario treated to this point in this chapter, we conduct a sensitivity analysis in order to test the importance of specific assumptions in the model to the GED results. Because prior research suggests health damages are particularly important (Burtraw et al. 1998; USEPA 1999; Muller and Mendelsohn 2007), the sensitivity analysis focuses on alternative ways to model health effects. Six alternative assumptions are used to generate additional scenarios. The first features an alternative concentration-response function relating long-term $PM_{2.5}$ exposures to adult mortality rates (Laden et al. 2006). In order to test the sensitivity of our results to the choice of the discount rate, the second and third scenarios employ 2 percent and 4 percent as alternative values for the social rate of time preference. In the fourth scenario, we apply the value of mortality risks uniformly regardless of the age of the persons exposed. In the fifth scenario, we apply the U.S. Environmental Protection Agency's preferred value for mortality risks: $620 for an additional 1/10,000 chance of death. This value is then tailored to the age of exposed people using the formula shown in chapter 3 (see equation 3.15). In the final scenario, we use the USEPA value of a statistical life ($6.2 million) and apply it uniformly to all ages.

Table 8-6 displays the results of the sensitivity analyses. Each of the six alternative scenarios employed in the sensitivity analysis display a range

TABLE 8-6
SENSITIVITY ANALYSIS OF GED BY POLLUTANT ($BILLION/YEAR)

Scenario	$PM_{2.5}$	PM_{10}	NO_x	NH_3	SO_2	VOCs	Total GED	Δ Base	GED/ GDP (%)
Discount Rate of 2%	26.5	7.2	7.5	14.9	29.3	17.1	102	−6%	1.0
Discount Rate of 4%	30.0	7.2	8.8	16.7	32.8	19.1	114	+5%	1.1
Uniform Age VSL	70.1	7.2	23.4	38.0	74.4	44.1	257	+136%	2.4
Laden (2006) Dose Response	61.3	7.2	20.4	34.3	67.8	35.9	227	+108%	2.1
USEPA VSL	85.2	7.2	28.9	47.2	92.2	50.3	311	+185%	2.9
USEPA Method	223	7.2	79.6	120	234	131	795	+630%	7.5

NOTE: VSL = value of statistical life. Baseline GED is $109 billion/yr.

of plausible values for key parameters and assumptions. Table 8-6 reveals that the GED is not sensitive to small changes in the discount rate (the first and second scenarios) because the discount rate has only a small effect on the value of premature deaths; the GED changes by only about 5 percent, given the perturbations to the discount rate explored here. However, GED is sensitive to the remaining assumptions tested. Using a uniform value of life regardless of age (uniform age value of statistical life [VSL]) increases GED by more than 130 percent. Using a more sensitive value for the concentration-response function between chronic exposure to $PM_{2.5}$ and adult mortality rates increases GED by about 100 percent. Specifically, substituting the relationship reported in Laden et al. (2006) for the association reported in Pope et al. (2002) yields aggregate damages of $227 billion (2.1 percent of GDP). Using the USEPA values for mortality risk increases the GED by 185 percent over the baseline. Finally, applying the $6.2 million VSL uniformly to populations of all ages increases the GED by 630 percent. In this final scenario, the GED of local air pollutants is valued at $795 billion, or 7.5 percent of GDP.

In addition to computing aggregate damages using the source-specific marginal damages, we run two additional experiments to estimate the damages from pollution. In all the experiments, we begin with the calculation of baseline damages corresponding to baseline levels of emissions (USEPA 2006). In what we call the Uniform Tonnage Experiment, one ton of a particular pollutant is added to all sources at once. Damages relative to baseline

TABLE 8-7
EXPERIMENTS USING AVERAGE DAMAGES

Scenario	$PM_{2.5}$	PM_{10}	NO_x	NH_3	SO_2	VOCs	GED ($billion/ year)
Marginal Damage	4,130	390	400	4,545	2,015	450	109
Uniform Tonnage Experiment	3,070	300	390	3,150	1,690	330	71.8
Equal Percentage Experiment	5,230	510	510	3,880	2,000	1,050	108

emissions are computed; the change in total damages is then divided by the total number of added tons. This produces an average damage per ton across all emission sources. In a second experiment, baseline emissions are increased by 1 percent for each pollutant at each source and compared with the baseline; we call this the Equal Percentage Experiment. Dividing the change in total damages yields an estimate of the average damage per ton weighted by the quantity of emissions from each source. In each case, we compute GED by multiplying total emissions times the average damage per ton for each pollutant.

Table 8-7 reports the results of these two experiments. The top row of table 8-7 reports the average of the marginal damage for each pollutant estimated using our source-specific approach. The shadow prices in the top row of table 8-7 are the means of the urban and rural prices reported in table 8-3. On adding one ton of one pollutant to all sources, the "Uniform Tonnage" runs, the average shadow prices are consistently lower than the values shown in the top row of table 8-7, because the uniform experiment does not capture the difference in marginal damages associated with emissions in urban versus rural areas. Each source is given equal weight. Because there are many more sources in rural locations than in urban locations, and because rural sources have relatively lower marginal damages than urban sources, the average prices from this experiment are lower. Applying the shadow prices derived from the Uniform Tonnage Experiment to compute aggregate damages results in a 34 percent decrease in GED from $109 billion to $71.8 billion.

Also shown in table 8-7 are the results of the Equal Percentage Experiment, where emissions are increased by 1 percent across all sources. The shadow prices derived from the Equal Percentage Experiment are greater than the Uniform Tonnage Experiment prices because less weight is given to remote rural sources that emit little pollution. The GED calculated using the Equal Percentage Experiment is $108 billion, which is very close to the baseline estimate of $109 billion. The similarity in the GED estimates using the Equal Percentage approach to the GED reported in the first row of table 8-7 indicates that approximating the source-specific marginal damages by using equal percentage changes in emissions is a viable approach to measuring the GED.

9

The Gross External Damages
from Air Pollution by Sector

In this chapter, we give a broad overview of the air pollution damages caused by each sector of the U.S. economy. In the next chapter we will present a more refined green accounting tool that attributes GED to each industry. Sectors are aggregates of industries. For example, the agriculture and forestry sector is composed of the crop, livestock, and forestry industries. We specifically measure and report the GED due to emissions from each sector in the U.S. economy identified by the U.S. Environmental Protection Agency, including mobile and residential sources, as well as the nineteen sectors employed in the North American Industry Classification System (NAICS).

We also compare the GED for each sector to the value added to the economy of that sector (U.S. Bureau of Economic Analysis 2009). This comparison provides a useful benchmark in terms of the external costs due to production in each sector relative to the value associated with production in that sector. The GED measures the pollution directly caused by the sector. VA measures the additional contribution of the sector to GDP. Although it would be interesting to examine the damages associated with GDP, we have not yet measured the GED associated with each input along the supply chain, so we cannot yet make this calculation. Hence, this analysis compares GED to VA.

We begin by computing the GED by sector. GED by sector is determined by measuring the emissions of each source in that sector and multiplying the emissions by the marginal damage caused by that specific source. The sector damages are the sum of GED across all the sources in that sector. Note that the total GED reported in the bottom row of table 9-1, $99 billion, is smaller by approximately 10 percent than the total GED reported in

TABLE 9-1
GROSS EXTERNAL DAMAGE ($BILLION/YEAR)
AND RATIO TO VALUE ADDED BY SECTOR

Sector	GED	% Total GED	GED/VA
Transportation and Warehousing[a]	33.8	31.0	[b]
Utilities	25.0	22.9	0.14
Agriculture and Forestry	12.2	11.2	0.13
Manufacturing	7.8	7.1	0.01
Construction	5.7	5.2	0.01
Residential Fuel Combustion	5.3	5.0	[b]
Waste Management and Remediation Services	3.7	3.4	0.01
Accommodation and Food Services	1.5	1.3	0.01
Mining	1.0	0.9	0.01
Arts, Entertainment, and Recreation	0.8	0.7	0.01
Retail Trade	0.6	0.6	0.00
Wholesale Trade	0.4	0.4	0.00
Other Services (except Public Administration)	0.4	0.3	0.00
Health Care and Social Assistance	0.1	0.1	0.00
Educational Services	0.1	0.1	0.00
Professional, Scientific, and Technical Services	0.0	0.0	0.00
Real Estate and Rental and Leasing	0.0	0.0	0.00
Information	0.0	0.0	0.00
Finance and Insurance	0.0	0.0	0.00
Management of Companies and Enterprises	0.0	0.0	0.00
Total GED	98.6	0.91	0.01

a. Transportation includes all mobile source emissions, including residential and commercial vehicles.

b. Value added not measured for residential and commercial transportation as well as residential combustion of fuels.

chapter 8. This difference stems from the inability to attribute some emissions from industrial sources to a particular sector in the economy. When the emissions from industrial nonpoint sources are included as shown in Table 9-3, the aggregate GED matches that reported in chapter 8.

The entire economy is divided into twenty aggregate sectors. Table 9-1 indicates that mobile sources—including both residential transport (by households) as well as commercial transport (by firms)—are responsible for the largest share of GED (31 percent). The total GED from mobile sources is $33.8 billion annually. The utility sector produces the next largest share (23 percent) or $25 billion damage annually. Taken together, mobile sources and utilities are responsible for more than one-half of total GED in the United States. Emissions from agricultural and forestry operations contribute the third largest share of GED (11 percent) or approximately $12 billion per year. The manufacturing sector is responsible for the fourth largest share of GED (7 percent), adding another $8 billion to the GED. Mobile sources, utilities, agriculture and forestry, and manufacturing caused nearly three-quarters of the GED in the United States in 2002.

Construction (5 percent or $5.7 billion), residential combustion of fuels (5 percent or $5.6 billion), and waste management (3 percent or $3.7 billion) all caused noticeable amounts of pollution damage. The remaining sectors are not important sources of air pollution damages.

Table 9-1 also reports the ratio between the GED and VA for each sector. The table shows that the agriculture-forestry and utility sectors are the two dirtiest sectors in terms of the fraction of air pollution damages per unit of value added. The agriculture-forestry sector has a GED-to-VA ratio of 0.13, and the utility sector has a GED-to-VA ratio of 0.14. On average, every dollar of value added contributed by the utility sector entails 14 cents worth of air pollution damage. Six other sectors show a GED-to-VA ratio of about 0.01. All of the remaining sectors show GED-to-VA ratios that are less than 0.01. It is important to note that because table 9-1 includes residential sources as part of the mobile source category, it is not possible to compare the GED produced by the transportation sector to a measure of value added. The same caveat holds for residential combustion sources.

Table 9-2 shows the damages due to CO_2 emissions in the United States according to broad source type. Note that the source categories in table 9-2 do not match the source categories reported in table 9-1. This discrepancy occurs because the U.S. Department of Energy is responsible for reporting CO_2 emissions, whereas the USEPA reports the emissions of the criteria pollutants. It is also important to notice that the total emissions reported in table 9-2 do not match the total CO_2 emissions reported in chapter 8. This is due to overlap between and among source types—principally residential, commercial, and transportation.

Table 9-2 shows that power generation is responsible for the largest quantity of CO_2 emissions and the greatest CO_2 damage. Specifically,

TABLE 9-2

GROSS EXTERNAL DAMAGES FROM CARBON DIOXIDE EMITTED
IN THE UNITED STATES ($BILLION/YEAR)

Source	Emissions (million tons CO_2)	GED^*_{low}	GED^*_{med}	GED^*_{high}
Residential	1,196	$4.8	$9.6	$34.7
Commercial	1,018	$4.1	$8.1	$29.5
Industrial	1,716	$6.9	$13.7	$49.7
Transportation	1,891	$7.6	$15.1	$54.8
Power Generation	2,271	$9.1	$18.2	$65.9

NOTE: Damage per ton values (Tol 2005): GED^*_{low} = $4/ton CO_2, GED^*_{med} = $8/ton CO_2, and GED^*_{high} = $29/ton CO_2.
SOURCE: U.S. Energy Information Administration 2008.

power producers emit nearly 2.3 billion tons of CO_2, which causes between $9 billion and $66 billion of damage (depending on the marginal damage attributed to a ton of CO_2). The transportation and industrial sectors contribute the next largest shares of total emissions and damages. In particular, transportation (mobile) sources generate 1.9 billion tons of CO_2, and the corresponding damage is estimated to be between $7.6 billion and $55 billion. Industrial sources produce 1.7 billion tons of CO_2, which translates into a damage of $7 billion to $50 billion. Residential sources generate nearly 1.2 billion tons of emissions and cause damage between $5 billion and $35 billion. And, finally, commercial sources emit 1.0 billion tons of CO_2 and cause damage of $4 billion to $30 billion.

Table 9-3 decomposes GED by broad source categories and by pollutant. Table 9-3 indicates that industrial point sources produce $31.9 billion in GED. Within this source category, most of the GED is due to emissions of SO_2, which generate $22 billion of damage. Most of the $22 billion in the GED due to industrial point sources is from coal-fired electric power plants, which are within the utility sector. Emissions of NO_x and $PM_{2.5}$ cause the next largest shares of the GED from industrial sources, with damages between $2.5 and $5 billion, respectively.

Industrial nonpoint sources cause $24.7 billion of GED. The industrial nonpoint sources tend to be small facilities that do not have tall smokestacks. The most harmful pollutants from the industrial nonpoint sources

TABLE 9-3
GED BY SOURCE TYPE AND POLLUTANT ($MILLION/YEAR)

Source Type	Pollutant						Total
	PM$_{2.5}$	PM$_{10}$	NO$_x$	SO$_2$	VOC	NH$_3$	
Agriculture	2,543	751	1	4	27	8,130	11,457
Residential Fuels	2,834	205	100	839	1,135	130	5,244
Light-Duty Vehicles	1,479	700	890	283	3,028	2,985	9,365
Light-Duty Trucks (Gas)	1,395	687	695	256	2,043	2,028	7,102
Highway Diesel	2,089	730	1,611	287	185	76	4,979
Off-Road Diesel	2,390	747	704	566	228	57	4,693
Off-Road Gas (HD)	1,710	697	256	74	2,479	141	5,356
Misc. Mobile	932	76	707	1,798	235	28	3,775
Industrial Nonpoint	8,360	1,919	601	4,619	7,673	1,505	24,677
Industrial Point	4,910	689	2,515	22,150	973	685	31,921
Total	28,642	7,202	8,080	30,876	18,006	15,765	108,569

are different from the industrial point sources. Specifically, the largest shares are due to PM$_{2.5}$ emissions ($8.4 billion) and VOCs ($7.7 billion), with another $4.6 billion of damage from discharges of SO$_2$. These damages stem from a wide variety of enterprises, including manufacturing installations, enterprises that use large amounts of solvents, publicly owned waste treatment facilities, and wholesale petroleum storage and distribution facilities.

The first two rows in table 9-3 encompass agricultural sources and residential fuel combustion. Agricultural sources generate $11.5 billion in GED.[1] The GED within this source group is roughly equally split between crop production and livestock production. However, in both cases most of the GED is due to emissions of ammonia (NH$_3$). In the case of livestock, NH$_3$ is emitted directly by animals. For crop production, NH$_3$ emissions emanate from fertilizer application.

Combustion of fuels by residential sources produces GED equal to $5.2 billion. This constitutes 5 percent of the GED. Emissions from residences stem from the fact that in order to produce heat and hot water, residences

---

1. In table 9-1 we report agriculture GED as $12.2 billion. The discrepancy with table 9-3 occurs because some of the agriculture sources are attributed to the nonroad mobile source categories in table 9-3.

burn heating oil (which is high in SO_2), wood (which produces relatively large amounts of $PM_{2.5}$), natural gas, and propane. Table 9-3 indicates that most of the damage caused by residences is due to emissions of $PM_{2.5}$ ($2.8 billion). Emissions of VOCs, SO_2, and PM_{10} also contribute appreciably to the GED produced by residential fuel combustion.

Table 9-3 also provides a detailed breakdown of mobile sources in the transportation sector. The three largest components of the GED produced by mobile sources are light-duty gasoline cars (and motorcycles), light-duty gasoline trucks, and off-road gasoline vehicles. The GED due to emissions from light-duty gasoline vehicles equals nearly $9.4 billion. These damages are made up mostly of NH_3, VOCs, and $PM_{2.5}$. For light-duty gasoline trucks, the GED is $7.1 billion. As with light-duty vehicles, these GED are mainly from NH_3, VOCs, and $PM_{2.5}$. Off-road heavy-duty gasoline vehicles produce $5.4 billion in GED. Emissions of VOC, $PM_{2.5}$, and PM_{10}, make up most of the GED from this source category. Off-road diesels, highway diesels, and miscellaneous mobile sources (railroads, aircraft, and marine vessels) form the last three categories. Highway diesel trucks generate $5 billion in GED. However, unlike gasoline-powered vehicles, diesel vehicles primarily emit NO_x and $PM_{2.5}$. This pattern holds for off-road diesel vehicles as well. These (typically heavy-duty) vehicles produce $4.7 billion in GED, and, like the highway diesels, the GED from this source group is largely due to emissions of $PM_{2.5}$ and NO_x. Again, the importance of fuel type on the mix of damages across pollutants is evident when looking at this vehicle class in table 9-3.

The final mobile source category includes railroads, marine vessels, and aircraft. The greatest share of the GED within this group is due to emissions from marine vessels (emissions while the vessels are in port). These vessels often run on bunker fuel, a high-energy, minimally refined fuel that emits large amounts of SO_2 and $PM_{2.5}$ when burned. Together, aircraft, railroads, and marine vessels produce GED of $3.8 billion.

Table 9-4 further decomposes the GED caused by these different source types according to whether the emissions occur in urban or rural locations. For the most part, damages caused by emissions in urban areas are considerably larger than emissions produced in rural areas. This is expected, given the findings in chapter 8 that indicate most of the GED is due to human health impacts. For example, the GED from light-duty vehicle emissions causes nearly six times more damage in urban areas than in rural areas.

TABLE 9-4
GED BY SOURCE TYPE AND LOCATION ($MILLION/YEAR)

Source Type	Location	
	Urban	Rural
Agriculture	5,520	5,904
Residential Fuels	4,058	1,187
Light-Duty Vehicles	8,013	1,378
Light-Duty Trucks	5,890	1,233
Highway Diesel Trucks	3,590	1,426
Off-Road Diesel	3,376	1,326
Off-Road Gasoline	4,219	1,149
Misc. Mobile	3,023	758
Industrial Area	20,685	4,018
Industrial Point	19,141	12,844
Total	77,515	31,223

However, some source types generate damages in both rural and urban areas. For instance, industrial point sources generate $19.1 billion of GED in urban areas and $12.8 billion of GED in rural areas. Many of the largest sources of industrial emissions are in rural areas, and as a result, damages per ton for this source group tend to be low. In addition, large industrial sources that are located in urban areas tend to have large smokestacks in order strive for compliance with ambient standards. Higher smokestacks, by sending emissions out of densely populated cities, keep damages per ton low and comparable with damages per ton from rural emissions. Another sector that generates significant rural damages is agriculture. More than 50 percent of the GED from agriculture is from rural sources. Of course, with agriculture, it is a little surprising that almost 50 percent of the air pollution damages are urban. The explanation is that, although there are fewer urban agricultural operations, damage from these facilities tends to be high per unit of output because there are large urban populations nearby.

10

Green Accounting, Including Air Pollution Damages in National Accounts

In this chapter we measure the contribution of each U.S. industry to GED and industry-specific GED to value added (VA). Industries are defined by the North American Industry Classification System developed by the U.S. Census Bureau. This approach to green accounting measures the GED of each industry using the emissions of each source in that industry. Multiplying the emissions from each source by marginal damages estimated in chapter 4 yields the GED by source. Summing across sources within each industry yields an industry-wide GED estimate. Using the source-specific marginal damages to value emission in tabulating the GED emphasizes the importance of the location of sources in each industry to the GED.

The analysis conducted in this chapter clearly reveals that the magnitude of the GED varies across industries. However, this variation may simply be due to differences in the size or scale of certain industries or to differing degrees of pollution intensity. To explore the latter dimension, we conduct industry-specific analyses of the relationship between GED and the value added. This approach mimics, on a much finer scale, the comparison executed in chapter 9 that compared the GED to VA for each sector. Scaling GED by VA explores the relative magnitude of the external costs produced by each industry compared to what it contributes to the economy. Looking at each industry reveals the vast heterogeneity within most economic sectors, from relatively clean to dirty industries. For example, manufacturing encompasses vastly distinct industrial processes; manufacturing includes both iron and steel manufacturing, which is relatively dirty, and microchip production, which is relatively clean.

In addition to providing a useful measurement of the impact of industry emissions, the findings reported herein may be used to develop a system of augmented production-based environmental accounts (Nordhaus and Kokkelenberg 1999; Muller, Mendelsohn, and Nordhaus 2011). Specifically, policymakers may use these data to move toward the computation of net national product. Economists have expressed concern that conventional measures of economic welfare, such as GDP, lack critical assessments of externalities and nonmarket activities associated with modern economies. For example, the value of leisure time and home production is omitted from GDP. In addition, environmental components of economic activity, such as depreciation of natural capital and the welfare impact of pollution, are not measured by GDP (Cairns 2000; Ayres and Kneese 1969). By including GED by industry, we demonstrate that it is possible to provide reliable measures of pollution in national accounts, a critical step toward the development of green accounting.

Although certain countries have taken steps toward measuring something akin to net national welfare, most efforts in this direction have focused on quantity-based accounts. For example, several countries in the European Union have developed statistical measures of forest resources, pollution emissions, and subsurface mineral assets (Peskin 1989; Repetto 1989; World Bank 1997; Gundimeda et al. 2007; Vardon et al. 2007). Although these are important steps in the right direction, they do not provide a sense of the magnitude of external costs relative to value added.

Another deficiency of tonnage-based accounting is that tonnage does not provide any sense of the role of location. Accounting based on tonnage implicitly assumes that the value of all emissions is equal, regardless of location. Although this assumption is appropriate for pollutants such as GHGs that cause the same marginal damage regardless of location, it is important to capture the spatial variation in marginal damage caused by local pollutants.

In order to consider these issues closely, we explore the GED due to emissions from the manufacturing sector and the electric power generation sector in great detail. For the manufacturing sector, we report the GED due to emissions of the ten industries whose emissions generate the greatest GED. This analysis highlights the heterogeneity of GED across industries within this sector. For electric power generation, we report the GED and the GED relative to value added for generators that employ each of the following fuel types: coal, oil, natural gas, coke, and wood biomass. The analysis highlights the difference in impact, on a GED per kilowatt hour (kwh) basis, across generators that employ these different fuels. Furthermore, we include the GED due to emissions of the principal GHGs in the analysis of the electric power sector. We extend the analysis to include GHGs in this case because of data availability about CO_2 emissions for power plants and because of the copious amounts of GHGs that are emitted by electric power generation.

We compute the GED by industry using the following methodology. As in the previous chapters, we use the USEPA's National Emission Inventory to provide the quantity (X) and source location (j) of every emission of each pollutant (s) tracked by the APEEP model in the contiguous United States (USEPA 2006). Each source is assigned to a six-digit industry code (i) that corresponds to the NAICS. As explicated in chapter 4, the APEEP model estimates the marginal damage of an emission of pollutant (s) from each location (j), $MD_{s,j}$. The GED for a source is calculated by multiplying the emissions $(X_{s,i,j})$ by the source location and pollutant-specific marginal damage $(MD_{s,j})$. The $GED_{s,i,j}$ attributed to source location (j) in industry (i) emitting pollutant (s) is shown in the following equation:

$$GED_{s,i,j} = MD_{s,j} \times X_{s,i,j} \qquad (10.1)$$

The total GED attributed to emissions of air pollution from industry (i) is the sum of damages across the six air pollutants covered by APEEP (s) and across all source locations (j).

$$GED_i = \Sigma_{s,j} \, (MD_{s,j} \times X_{s,i,j}) \qquad (10.2)$$

For each six-digit NAICS industry, we measure the ratio of GED_i to VA_i (U.S. Bureau of Economic Analysis 2009). The damage due to emissions of GHGs is calculated in a similar fashion using the social cost of carbon and the methodology described in chapters 8 and 9.

In this chapter we report the GED according to two modeling scenarios. In the first scenario, we compute GED^A in which we employ a VSL of approximately \$2 million, which is equivalent to assuming a change in annual mortality risks of 0.00001 is worth \$200 per year. In this scenario, the mortality value is assumed to vary depending on years of life

TABLE 10-1
GROSS EXTERNAL DAMAGE BY INDUSTRY:
INDUSTRIES WITH THE LARGEST GED ($BILLION/YEAR)

Industry	GED^A	GED^B
Coal-fired Electric Power Generation	18.7	142.0
Crop Production	6.0	41.3
Livestock Production	5.4	40.6
Highway, Street, and Bridge Construction	5.1	32.4
Truck Transportation	3.2	27.3
Water Transportation	2.4	19.4
Solid Waste Combustion and Incinerators	1.7	12.7
Petroleum Refineries	1.6	11.6
Food Service Contractors	1.5	11.1
Landscaping Services	1.4	10.3

NOTE: GED^A employs a VSL of $2 million, and GED^B employs a VSL of $6.2 million.

remaining, as described in chapter 3. GED^A is the default case in chapter 8. In the second scenario, we compute GED^B using a VSL of $6.2 million that assumes a change in mortality risk of 0.00001 is worth $620 (the value used by USEPA), and the assumption that the VSL applies to all age cohorts uniformly. GED^B is the final scenario explored in the sensitivity analysis in chapter 8.

Table 10-1 reports the GED for the ten industries that generate the largest GED. Coal-fired power generation produces, by far, the greatest GED under both modeling scenarios of $19 billion and $142 billion, respectively. Crop production, livestock production, and transportation-based construction activities generate the next largest GED. For each of these industries, GED^A is near $5 billion and GED^B is between $32 billion and $41 billion. Other important industries that produce large GED include truck transportation, water transportation, solid waste combustion and incinerators, petroleum refineries, food service contractors, and landscaping services.

Note that of the ten most polluting sectors, only one (petroleum refineries) is in manufacturing. Table 10-2 shows the ten industries just within the manufacturing sector that generate the greatest GED. The five worst polluters in the manufacturing sector are petroleum refineries ($1.6 billion), iron

TABLE 10-2

GROSS EXTERNAL DAMAGES AND VALUE ADDED
FROM THE U.S. MANUFACTURING SECTOR ($BILLION/YEAR)

Industry	GED^A	GED^B	% Mfg. GED	GED^A/VA	GED^B/VA
Petroleum Refineries	1.6	11.6	20	0.06	0.43
Iron and Steel Mills	0.5	4.0	7	0.03	0.23
Cement Mfg.	0.3	2.4	4	0.07	0.54
Adhesive Mfg.	0.3	2.0	3	0.08	0.56
Paper Mills	0.2	1.7	3	0.01	0.07
Petrochemical Mfg.	0.2	1.5	3	0.04	0.27
Automobile Mfg.	0.2	1.4	3	0.01	0.05
Coke Ovens	0.2	1.4	2	0.39	2.86
Pharmaceutical Prepa-ration Mfg.	0.2	1.3	2	0.00	0.02
Basic Organic Chemical Mfg.	0.1	1.1	2	0.01	0.06

NOTE: GED^A employs a VSL of $2 million, and GED^B employs a VSL of $6.2 million.

and steel mills ($0.5 billion), cement manufacturing ($0.3 billion), adhesive manufacturing ($0.3 billion), and paper mills ($0.2 billion). Table 10-2 also displays the ratio of GED to VA for these industries. One of the interesting results in this table is that the GED^A/VA ratio for manufacturing industries is relatively low. Only coke ovens (at 0.39) have a GED^A/VA ratio greater than 0.10. Note, however, that with GED^B, six industries have a GED^B/VA ratio that is greater than 0.10. These industries include coke ovens, iron and steel mills, adhesive manufacturing, petroleum refineries, petrochemical manufacturing, and cement manufacturing.

Table 10-3 explores the GED for the electric power generation sector. This table focuses on facilities that burn fossil fuels and wood biomass, because these fuels generate the greatest air pollution damages. In contrast, nuclear (during regular operations), wind, and hydroelectric power generators produce negligible air pollution damage and therefore are not included in table 10-3. Table 10-3 indicates that coal-fired power generation produces the greatest GED, about $19 billion. The next largest GED is produced by oil-fired generators, which cause GED of nearly $600 million.

TABLE 10-3
GED FROM THE U.S. ELECTRIC POWER GENERATION SECTOR

Fuel Type	GED ($million/ year)	GED/kwh (¢/kwh)	GED* ($million/ year)	GED*/kwh (¢/kwh)
Coal	18,700	0.97	34,200	1.77
	(142,000)	(7.35)	(158,000)	(8.15)
Oil	590	0.75	1,320	1.68
	(4,880)	(6.19)	(5,600)	(7.12)
Coke	29	0.18	29	0.18
	(210)	(1.32)	(210)	(1.32)
Natural Gas	300	0.04	3,330	0.48
	(2,270)	(0.33)	(5,300)	(0.77)
Wood Biomass	5	0.04	5 (31)	0.04
	(31)	(0.33)		(0.33)
Average GED/kwh		0.72		1.42
		(5.45)		(6.16)

Note: GED^A is the first number, and GED^B is in parentheses. GED^A employs a VSL of $2 million, and GED^B employs a VSL of $6.2 million. GED* includes damages from CO_2 emissions, valued at $8/tCO_2$.

Natural gas is much cleaner; the GED produced by natural gas–fired power plants is just $300 million. Coke and wood biomass produce considerably smaller GED, primarily because they are a relatively minor fraction of total power generation in the United States. For coke-fired facilities, the GED is $30 million, and for wood biomass plants the GED is $5 million.

Table 10-3 also reports the GED on a per-kilowatt-hour basis. Coal-and oil-based power cause the greatest harm per kilowatt hour; the GED/kwh is 1¢/kwh for coal and 0.8¢/kwh for oil. Power produced by burning coke generates GED/kwh of 0.2¢/kwh. Interestingly, the GED/kwh for natural gas and wood biomass are similar at 0.04¢/kwh and 0.04¢/kwh, respectively. The generation-weighted average GED/kwh for all of these fuels is 0.72¢/kwh. This average is heavily influenced by the GED/kwh for coal, because nearly 50 percent of net power generation in the United States in 2002 was produced by burning coal. Table 10-3 reports both GED^A and GED^B values. The higher values associated with GED^B lead to much higher estimates of GED. The generation-weighted average GED/kwh increases from 0.72¢/kwh to 5.45¢/kwh.

Table 10-3 also reports GED*, which includes damages due to emissions of CO_2 from each of the facility types. Table 10-3 values CO_2 at \$8/ ton (or approximately \$29/tC). When emissions of CO_2 are included in the analysis, coal-fired generation causes GED* of \$34 billion and GED*/ kwh of 1.77¢/kwh. When we employ the GED^B methodology, the GED*/ kwh increases to 8.15¢/kwh. This suggests that when using the modeling assumptions that produce GED^B, the external costs due to air pollution and CO_2 emissions from coal-fired electric power generation were comparable in 2002 to the national average price for electricity. If consumers of coal-fired electric power faced these external costs, it is likely that demand would change considerably, although further modeling is necessary to determine by how much and how quickly demand for power would change if consumers faced these external costs.

Perhaps the most interesting result in table 10-3 is the change from GED/kwh to GED*/kwh for natural gas and biomass. For biomass, the GED/kwh and the GED*/kwh are both 0.05¢/kwh because the U.S. Department of Energy (the source of the CO_2 emission inventory) reports CO_2 emissions as being zero for this fuel type. This reflects the agency's carbon-neutrality assumption for biomass. For natural gas, the GED/kwh increases from 0.04¢/kwh to 0.48¢/kwh when CO_2 emissions are included in the accounting domain. This very large change emphasizes that natural gas is a clean fuel to produce power in terms of local air pollution. However, natural gas is not quite as clean when CO_2 damages are included.

Table 10-4 compares the GED to value added for each industry in the United States, and reports the eleven industries with the largest GED-to-VA ratio. Topping the list in table 10-4 is solid waste combustion, with a GED-to-VA ratio of between 2.3 to 17.4, depending on modeling assumptions. The next industry is petroleum-fired power generation, which shows a GED-to-VA ratio that ranges from 1.7 to 13.8. Following oil-fired power, the sewage treatment industry has a GED-to-VA ratio of between 1.6 and 12.5. For each of these industries, the air pollution damage far exceeds the value added. Next in table 10-4 is coal-fired power generation, which has a GED-to-VA ratio that is between 0.8 and 5.8. The remaining industries in table 10-4 have a GED-to-VA ratio that ranges between 0.2 and 0.8 when using the GED^A method and between 1.8 and 4.7 using GED^B.

TABLE 10-4

GED RELATIVE TO VALUE ADDED BY INDUSTRY ($MILLION/YEAR)

Industry	GED^A/VA	GED^B/VA
Solid Waste Combustion and Incinerators	2.3	17.4
Petroleum-fired Electric Power Generation	1.7	13.8
Sewage Treatment Facilities	1.6	12.5
Coal-fired Electric Power Generation	0.8	5.8
Dimension Stone Mining and Quarrying	0.8	4.7
Marinas	0.5	3.9
Coke Ovens	0.5	3.5
Steam and Air Conditioning Supply	0.4	2.8
Water Transportation	0.3	2.5
Sugarcane Mills	0.2	2.0
Carbon Black Mfg.	0.2	1.8

NOTE: GED^A employs a VSL of $2 million, and GED^B employs a VSL of $6.2 million.

Two important themes emerge from table 10-4. One-quarter of the industries in table 10-4 are in the utility sector. This suggests that utilities (especially fossil-fuel power generation) are particularly pollution intensive relative to their value added. Also of note is that only two industries from the manufacturing sector appear in table 10-4: coke ovens and sugarcane mills. In transport, only water transportation shows up in table 10-4. This highlights the importance of scaling the GED by value added, because chapter 9 reported that both manufacturing and transportation produce large GED.

The fact that air pollution damage exceeds value added in some industries suggests there are serious regulatory problems in those industries. It is likely that the air pollution is not sufficiently regulated. Stricter regulation would reduce the amount of damage (GED) and raise output prices, increasing value added. Of course, stricter regulation may reduce the competitiveness of these industries and would likely shrink output. The findings, however, should not be interpreted as suggesting that these industries necessarily should be eliminated. Improved regulations could well be all that is required to reduce the GED/VA ratio to reasonable levels.

It is interesting that two of the industries with the highest GED/VA ratio are waste management industries (sewage treatment and waste incineration). The analysis suggests that the regulations that govern these two industries have not properly accounted for the air pollution damage. The government needs to invest in integrated pollution management to examine all the damage types (air, water, soils) simultaneously. The integrated pollution management analysis needs to determine whether these treatment facilities have taken wastes that are initially a water and solid waste problem and turned the wastes into a more harmful air pollution problem. But this determination cannot be made until the externalities associated with water and solid waste are properly accounted for in the analysis.

Conclusion

In this book, we argue that air pollution policy in the United States is not yet efficient because it does not fully incorporate marginal damages into regulatory design. By equating marginal cost with marginal damage, a fully efficient regulatory scheme can be designed. Why should the United States aspire to an efficient air pollution policy regime? An efficient regulatory program produces the greatest good for the greatest number of people. Efficiency maximizes social welfare. From an economist's perspective, it is the final goal of regulatory reform. It will return the greatest social benefit for the abatement costs incurred by each regulation.

Simply moving from current rules directly to an efficient system would be ideal. But it is also possible to use efficiency principles to guide smaller but perhaps more realistic efforts toward an efficient regulatory program. Given the current mix of regulatory standards and cost-effective cap-and-trade regimes, an efficient plan provides a guide; comparing current marginal damages to marginal abatement costs reveals which regulatory reforms would lead to the greatest return. Such reforms may be structural, moving toward a fully efficient set of policies, or incremental. If undertaking piecemeal reforms, policymakers should focus changes on those sources and pollutants with the largest difference between marginal damage and marginal cost. This yields the greatest return on incremental investments in abatement.

In addition to promoting the idea of an efficient regulatory system, we demonstrate that such a change is possible. The missing element in regulatory design has been information on source-specific marginal damages. This book demonstrates that it is possible to estimate marginal damage. IAMs have long been used in air pollution research to connect emissions to concentrations, to physical effects, and to aggregate damage. We show that these same IAMs can measure the marginal damages of air pollution in the United States. By incrementally increasing emissions one at a time, we show that IAMs can be used to estimate source-specific marginal damage. We calculate the marginal damage for ten thousand sources and six major air pollutants in the United States, in order to show that it is possible to estimate all sixty thousand marginal damages in a computationally feasible manner. The analysis reveals that marginal damage varies by pollutant and by location; emissions of $PM_{2.5}$, NH_3, and SO_2 tend to be the most harmful, and emissions in cities tend to be more harmful than discharges in rural areas. Policies that fail to take into account these variations will not be efficient. Because current regulatory schemes do not take into account these variations, they are not yet efficient. The analysis also demonstrates that the variation in the marginal damages is quite large.

Substantial efficiency gains are possible in current air pollution regulatory regimes. These opportunities for efficiency gains stem from instances where the marginal damages and marginal abatement costs are dissimilar. In most cases where large efficiency gains are possible, marginal damages are far greater than marginal costs. We argue that such sources should be a high priority for regulatory reform.

The analyses in this book point out many important policy implications for regulatory reform. The examples focus on air pollution policies in the United States, but in principle the reforms pertain to almost all pollutants and to every country in the world. Our findings suggest that, despite the considerable progress that has been achieved controlling air pollution in the United States, remaining emissions still cause appreciable damage. We estimate current emissions cause between $100 billion and $800 billion in damage annually, depending on modeling assumptions.

A certain amount of damage cannot be avoided, because the cost of completely eliminating pollution eventually exceeds the benefit of abatement. The United States already spends vast resources on pollution abatement. The key in arguing for reforms is not blanket reductions in tonnage, but rather focused reductions of very high marginal damage emissions. Specifically, regulators need to examine the marginal damage and marginal cost of many sources and pollutants that are currently regulated. They should then focus on loosening regulations on emissions with high net marginal costs (marginal abatement cost exceeding marginal damage) and tightening regulations with high net marginal damage (marginal damage exceeds marginal cost). These reforms would yield very large gains.

One specific case (see chapter 6), the emission of sulfur dioxide from power plants, is very revealing. Moving from a cap-and-trade system that places the same value on every ton to a trading system that weights each ton by its marginal damage could generate substantial efficiency gains per year. By taking into account the variation in marginal damages, the cap-and-trade system could lead to much larger welfare gains. In the case of sulfur dioxide produced by power plants, the savings would *not* be due to lower abatement costs. In fact, the efficient program would slightly increase abatement costs of power plants. The gains stem from the reduction of damage. By focusing abatement on high marginal damage emissions, the efficient program gets a much bigger bang for the buck; damage is reduced by far more than abatement cost increases.

Another revealing example concerns the movement from standards to cap and trade that occurred in the 1990s. The SO_2 trading program across utilities allowed power plants to trade with each other ton for ton. The literature estimates that this resulted in a reduction of abatement costs worth between $0.7 and $2.1 billion annually (Henry et al. 2011). However, examining the damage caused by emissions before and after the trading reveals that the trading program increased damage between $1.5 and $5.4 billion annually. In other words, because the program failed to take damages into account, the SO_2 trading program may have actually *reduced* social welfare. It appears that the program inadvertently caused power plants to abate low-damage emissions in order to increase high-damage emissions. Hence, regulatory reforms that ignore marginal damages can backfire.

Another policy conclusion of this analysis is that regulators should base regulations on the damages caused by air pollution rather than simply on the tonnage. By focusing resources on reducing damages, regulations will become more efficient. Focusing on damage rather than tonnage generally implies that reducing emissions from urban areas is more important than reducing emissions from rural areas. This principle is especially true for ground-level emissions of particularly harmful pollutants such as $PM_{2.5}$ and NH_3. These two pollutants seem to cause especially high damages, and yet many sources of these pollutants are often not directly regulated by federal policy. In contrast, we find evidence that suggests regulations are too strict for many ground-level NO_x emissions in urban areas where the nonlinear atmospheric chemistry of ozone formation suggests these emissions often cause little net harm.

Our results also raise questions about certain industries with surprisingly high GED/VA ratios. Sewage treatment plants, solid waste incineration facilities, and oil-fired power plants all cause air pollution damage that exceeds the net value of their production to the U.S. economy. Coal-fired power plants have a GED equal to 80 percent of value added. These findings imply that these industries are currently a drag on the economy. However, current measures of economic performance such as GDP do not reflect this, because they fail to measure the GED and other nonmarket costs. Of course, that does not imply that the industries should be shut down. But it does imply that the industries are grossly underregulated. Air pollution emissions from all of these industries need to be reduced. This would lower the GED from each industry. However, it would also lead to higher output prices, which would increase the VA of these industries. Of course, the higher prices would reduce demand, but these changes in output would be desirable. The tighter regulations would force each industry to reduce the environmental cost of their production and level the playing field with competitors. For example, the price of electricity from coal would rise, allowing cleaner fuels such as natural gas or renewable fuels to more fairly compete.

An extension of the effort to include marginal damage is that it allows regulators to set more equivalent regulations across pollutants. This study only compares air pollutants. But in principle, the work could be extended to compare water pollution and solid waste as well. A useful extension of this work would allow regulators to explore fully integrated pollution management. The analysis of industries suggests that such an extension would be of immediate value. Two of the worst industries are pollution control industries. Waste incineration plants currently create more air pollution damage than reported VA. Sewage treatment plants currently generate more air pollution damage than the water treatment fees that they collect. Both waste incineration plants and sewage treatment plants should be redesigned to emit far less air pollution. Integrated pollution management could determine what levels of air pollution abatement relative to water and solid waste pollution would be desirable.

Many important questions remain to be answered about the precise design of efficient air pollution regulatory regimes. How spatially detailed should the policies be? Should they vary by day or season? How will firms and industries react to the new policies? How will abatement expenditures change across firms? Will the system encourage polluters to move to low-damage sites? Would such migration be desirable? How often should the regulations be updated to take into account changes in marginal damage? Can efficient policies be expanded to water and solid waste pollution? Can the approach become the foundation for integrated pollution management? We believe that the time has come and that the tools are available to address these questions.

References

Abbey, D. E., F. Peterson, P. K. Mills, and W. L. Beeson. 1993. Long-term Ambient Concentrations of Total Suspended Particulates, Ozone, and Sulfur Dioxide and Respiratory Symptoms in a Nonsmoking Population. *Archives of Environmental Health* 48:33–46.

Abdel-Aziz, A., and H. Christopher Frey. 2004. Propagation of Uncertainty in Hourly Utility NOx Emissions through a Photochemical Grid Air Quality Model: A Case Study for the Charlotte, NC, Modeling Domain. *Environmental Science and Technology* 38 (7): 2153–60.

Atkinson, S. E., and T. H. Tietenberg. 1982. The Empirical Properties of Two Classes of Designs for Transferable Discharge Permit Markets. *Journal of Environmental Economics and Management* 9:101–21.

Atteraas, L., and S. Haagenrud. 1982. Atmospheric Corrosion Testing in Norway. In *Atmospheric Corrosion*, ed. W. H. Ailor, 873–92. New York: Wiley InterScience.

Ayres, Robert U., and Allen V. Kneese. 1969. Production, Consumption, and Externalities. *American Economic Review* 59:282–97.

Baedecker, P.A., 1990. Dose-Response Functions for the Chemical Erosion of Carbonate Stone. In *NAPAP State of Science and Technology Report*, vol. 3. Washington, DC: National Acid Precipitation Assessment Program.

Baumol, W. J., and W. E. Oates. 1988. *The Theory of Environmental Policy*. 2nd ed. Cambridge: Cambridge University Press.

Bell, M. L. A., S. McDermott, L. Zeger, J. M. Samet, and F. Dominici. 2004. Ozone and Short-Term Mortality in 95 US Urban Communities, 1987–2000. *Journal of the American Medical Association* 17:2372–78.

Briggs, G. A. 1969. Plume Rise. USAEC Critical Review Series, TID–25075. Springfield, VA: National Technical Information Service.

———. 1971. Some Recent Analyses of Plume Rise Observations. In *Proceedings of the Second International Clean Air Congress*, ed. H. M. Englund and W. T. Berry, 1029–32. New York: Academic Press.

———. 1975. Plume Rise Predictions. In *Lectures on Air Pollution and Environmental Impact Analysis*, ed. Duane A. Haugen. Boston: American Meteorological Society.

Burnett, R. T., M. Smith-Doiron, D. Stieb, S. Cakmak, and J. R. Brook. 1999. Effects of Particulate and Gaseous Air Pollution on Cardiorespiratory Hospitalizations. *Archives of Environmental Health* 54 (2): 130–39.

Burtraw, D., A. Krupnick, E. Mansur, D. Austin, and D. Farrell. 1998. Costs and Benefits of Reducing Air Pollutants Related to Acid Rain. *Contemporary Economic Policy* 16 (4): 379–400.

Byun, D. W., and K. L. Schere. 2006. Review of the Governing Equations, Computational Algorithms, and Other Components of the Models-3 Community Multiscale Air Quality (CMAQ) Modeling System. *Applied Mechanics Reviews* 59 (2): 51–77.

Cairns, Robert D. 2000. Accounting for Resource Depletion: A Microeconomic Approach. *Review of Income and Wealth* 46 (1): 21–31.

Carlson, Curtis, Dallas Burtraw, Maureen L. Cropper, and Karen L. Palmer. 2000. Sulfur Dioxide Control by Electric Utilities: What Are the Gains from Trade? *Journal of Political Economy* 108 (6): 1292–1326.

Chestnut, L. G., and R. L. Dennis. 1997. Economic Benefits of Improvements in Visibility: Acid Rain Provisions of the 1990 Clean Air Act Amendments. *Journal of the Air and Waste Management Association* 47:395–402.

Chestnut, Lauraine G., and Robert D. Rowe. 1990. Preservation Values for Visibility Protection at National Parks. Working Paper, University of Colorado Center for Economic Analysis, Boulder.

Dales, J. H. 1968. *Pollution, Property and Prices: An Essay in Policy-making and Economics.* Toronto: University of Toronto Press.

Fann, N., C. M. Fulcher, B. J. Hubbell. 2009. The Influence of Location, Source, and Emission Type in Estimates of the Human Health Benefits of Reducing a Ton of Air Pollution. *Air Quality Atmosphere and Health.* 2:169-176.

Farrow, R. S., M. T. Schultz, P. Celikkol, and G. L. Van Houtven. 2005. Pollution Trading in Water Quality Limited Areas: Use of Benefits Assessment and Cost Effective Trading Ratios. *Land Economics* 81 (2): 191–205.

Faustmann, M. 1849. Calculation of the Value Which Forestland and Immature Stands Possess for Forestry. Reprinted in *Journal of Forest Economics* 1 (1): 7–44 (1995).

Freeman, A. Myrick, III. 1982. *Air and Water Pollution Control: A Benefit–Cost Analysis.* New York: John Wiley and Sons.

———. 2003. *The Measurement of Environmental and Resource Values.* 2nd ed. Washington, DC: RFF Press.

Frey, H. Christopher, and Song Li. 2003. Methods for Quantifying Variability and Uncertainty in AP-42 Emission Factors: Case Studies for Natural Gas-Fueled Engines. *Journal of the Air and Waste Management Association* 53 (12): 1436–47.

Frey, H. Christopher, and Junyu Zheng. 2002. Quantification of Variability and Uncertainty in Air Pollution Emission Inventories: Method and Case Study for Utility NO$_x$ Emissions. *Journal of the Air and Waste Management Association* 52 (9): 1083–95.

Goulder, L. H., ed. 2002. *Environmental Policy Making in Economies with Prior Tax Distortions.* Cheltenham, UK: Edward Elgar.

Grosjean, Daniel, and John H. Seinfeld. 1989. Parameterization of the Formation Potential of Secondary Organic Aerosols. *Atmospheric Environment* 23:1733–47.

Gundimeda, Haripriya, Pavan Sukhdev, Rajiv K. Sinha, and Sanjav Sanyal. 2007. Natural Resource Accounting for Indian States—Illustrating the Case for Forest Resources. *Ecological Economics* 61:635–49.

Haynie, F. H., J. W. Spence, and F. W. Lipfert. 1989. Development and Evaluation of an Atmospheric Damage Function for Galvanized Steel. U.S. Environmental Protection Agency, Research Triangle Park, NC.

Henry, D., N. Muller, and R. Mendelsohn 2011. The Social Cost of Trading: Measuring the Increased Damages from Sulfur Dioxide Trading in the United States. *Journal of Policy Analysis and Management* 30: 598–612.

Hogsett, W. E., J. E. Weber, D. Tingey, A. Herstrom, E. H. Lee, and J. A. Laurence. 1997. Environmental Auditing: An Approach for Characterizing Tropospheric Ozone Risk to Forests. *Environmental Management* 21 (1): 105–20.

International Cooperative Programme on Effects on Materials including Historic and Cultural Monuments (ICP). 2012. http://www.corr-institute.se/ICP-Materials/web/page.aspx?refid=12

Kengen, S. 1997. *Forest Valuation for Decision-Making: Lessons of Experience and Proposals for Improvement.* Rome, Italy: Food and Agriculture Organization of the United Nations.

Keohane, Nathaniel O. 2006. Cost Savings from Allowance Trading in the 1990 Clean Air Act: Estimates from a Choice-Based Model. In *Moving to Markets in Environmental Regulation: Lessons from Twenty Years of Experience*, ed. Charles E. Kolstad and Jody Freeman, 194–229. Oxford: Oxford University Press.

Klaassen, G. A. J., F. R. Førsund, and M. Amann. 1994. Emissions Trading in Europe with an Exchange Rate. *Environmental and Resource Economics* 4:305–30.

Klemm, R. J., and R. Mason. 2003. Replication of Reanalysis of Harvard Six-City Mortality Study. In *Revised Analyses of Time-Series Studies of Air Pollution and Health. Health.* Boston: Health Effects Institute.

Krupnick, A. J., W. E. Oates, and E. Van de Verg. 1983. On Marketable Air Pollution Permits: The Case for a System of Pollution Offsets. *Journal of Environmental Economics and Management* 10:233–47.

Kuykendal, William B., Jennifer Filipowski, and Thomas B. McMullen. 2006. A Quantitative Analysis of the Uncertainty of Emissions Data: A Limited Study. http://www.epa.gov/ttn/chief/conference/ei15/session13/kuykendal.pdf.

Laden, F., J. Schwartz, F. E. Speizer, and D. W. Dockery. 2006. Reduction in Fine Particulate Air Pollution and Mortality: Extended Follow-up of the Harvard Six Cities Study. *American Journal of Respiratory and Critical Care Medicine* 173:667–72.

Lesser, V. M., J. O. Rawlings, S. E. Spruill, and M. C. Somerville. 1990. Ozone Effects on Agricultural Crops: Statistical Methodologies and Estimated Dose-Response Relationships. *Crop Science* 30:148–55.

Levy, J. I., L.K. Baxter, J. Schwartz. 2009. Uncertainty and Variability in Health-Related Damages from Coal-fired Power Plants in the United States. *Risk Analysis.* DOI: 10.1111/j.1539-6924.2009.01227.

Loehman, E., and D. Boldt. 1990. *Valuing Gains and Losses in Visibility and Health with Contingent Valuation*. Unpublished Report.

Mauzerall, D., B. Sultan, N. Kim, and D. F. Bradford. 2005. NO_x Emissions from Large Point Sources: Variability in Ozone Production, Resulting Health Damages and Economic Costs. *Atmospheric Environment* 39:2851–66.

McClelland, G. H., W. D. Schulze, D. Waldman, D. Schenk, J. R. Irwin, T. Stewart, L. Deck, and M. A. Thayer. 1993. Valuing Eastern Visibility: A Field Test of the Contingent Valuation Method. In *Visibility of Fine Particles, Transactions of the Air and Waste Management Association*, ed. C.V. Mathaj, 647–58. Pittsburgh: Air and Waste Management Association.

McDonnell, D. E. Abbey, N. Nishino, and M. D. Lebowitz. 1999. Long-Term Ambient Ozone Concentration and the Incidence of Asthma in Non-Smoking Adults: The Ahsmog Study. *Environmental Research* 80 (2, pt. 1): 110–21.

Mendelsohn, Robert. 1980. An Economic Analysis of Air Pollution from Coal-Fired Power Plants. *Journal of Environmental Economics and Management* 7:30–43.

———. 1984. Endogenous Technical Change and Environmental Regulation. *Journal of Environmental Economics and Management* 11:202–7.

Mendelsohn, Robert, and Sheila M. Olmstead. 2009. The Economic Valuation of Environmental Amenities and Disamenities: Methods and Applications. *Annual Review of Environment and Resources* 34 (Nov.): 325–47.

Montgomery, W. D. 1972. Markets in Licenses and Efficient Pollution Control Programs. *Journal of Economic Theory* 5 (3): 395–418.

Moolgavkar, Suresh H. 2000. Air Pollution and Hospital Admissions for Chronic Obstructive Pulmonary Disease in Three Metropolitan Areas in the United States. *Inhalation Toxicology* 12:75–90.

Mrozek, J. R., and L. O. Taylor. 2002. What Determines the Value of Life? A Meta–Analysis. *Journal of Policy Analysis and Management* 21 (2): 253–70.

Muller, Nicholas Z. 2011. "Linking Policy to Statistical Uncertainty in Air Pollution Damages." *The B.E. Press Journal of Economic Analysis & Policy*. Vol. 11 : Iss. 1 (Contributions), Article 32.

———. 2012. https://sites.google.com/site/nickmullershomepage/home/ap2-data.

Muller, Nicholas Z., and Robert Mendelsohn. 2007. Measuring the Damages from Air Pollution in the United States. *Journal of Environmental Economics and Management* 54:1–14. Supplementary data appendix: http://www.sciencedirect.com/science/journal/00950696/54/1

———. 2009. Efficient Pollution Regulation: Getting the Prices Right. *American Economic Review* 99 (5): 1714–39. Supplementary data appendix: http://dx.doi.org/10.1257/aer.102.1.1

———. 2012. Efficient Pollution Regulation: Getting the Prices Right: Comment: Reply. *American Economic Review* 102(1): 608–612.

Muller, Nicholas Z., Robert Mendelsohn, and William Nordhaus. 2011. Environmental Accounting: Methods with an Application to the United States Economy. *American Economic Review* 101:1–30.

Nordhaus, W. D. 1992. An Optimal Transition Path for Controlling Greenhouse Gases. *Science* 258:1315–19.

———. 2008. *A Question of Balance: Economic Models of Global Warming.* New Haven, CT: Yale University Press.

Nordhaus, W. D., and Edward Kokkelenberg, eds. 1999. *Nature's Numbers.* Washington, DC: National Academy Press.

Pasquill, F. 1961. The Estimation of the Dispersion of Windborne Material. *Meteorology Magazine* 90 (1063): 33–49.

Peskin, Henry M. 1989. A Proposed Environmental Accounts Framework. In *Environmental Accounting for Sustainability*, ed. Y.J. Ahmed, S. El Serafy, and E. Lutz. Washington, DC: World Bank.

Pope, C. Arden, R. T. Burnett, M. J. Thun, E. E. Calle, D. Krewski, K. Ito, and G. D. Thurston. 2002. Lung Cancer, Cardiopulmonary Mortality, and Long-Term Exposure to Fine Particulate Air Pollution. *Journal of the American Medical Association* 287:1132–41.

Pye, J. M. 1988. Impact of Ozone on the Growth and Yield of Trees: A Review. *Journal of Environmental Quality* 17:347–60.

Rabl, A., and J. V. Spadaro. 1999. "Damages and Costs of Air Pollution: An Analysis of Uncertainties." *Environment International* 25(1): 29–46.

Reich, P. B., 1987. Quantifying Plant Response to Ozone: A Unifying Theory. *Tree Physiology* 3:63–91.

Repetto, Robert. 1989. *Wasting Assets: Natural Resources in the National Income Accounts.* Washington, DC: World Resources Institute.

Russell, A., and R. Dennis. 2000. NARSTO Critical Review of Photochemical Models and Modeling. *Atmospheric Environment* 34:2284–2324.

Schmalensee, Richard L., Paul L. Joskow, A. Denny Ellerman, Juan Pablo Montero, and Elizabeth M. Bailey. 1998. An Interim Evaluation of Sulfur Dioxide Emissions Trading. *Journal of Economic Perspectives* 12 (3): 53–68.

Schwartz, J., and R. Morris. 1995. Air Pollution and Hospital Emergency Room Visits for Asthma in Seattle. *American Review of Respiratory Disease* 142:23–35.

Seinfeld, J. H., and S. N. Pandis. 1998. *Atmospheric Chemistry and Physics.* New York: John Wiley and Sons.

Sheppard, L., D. Levy, G. Norris, T. V. Larson, and J. Q. Koenig. 1999. Effects of Ambient Air Pollution on Non-elderly Asthma Hospital Admissions in Seattle, Washington, 1987–1994. *Epidemiology* 10 (1): 23–30.

Sohngen, B., and R. Mendelsohn. 1998. Valuing the Market Impact of Large-Scale Ecological Change: The Effect of Climate Change on US Timber. *American Economic Review* 88:686–710.

Steib, D. M., R. T. Burnett, R. C. Beveridge, and J. R. Brook. 1996. Association between Ozone and Asthma Emergency Department Visits in St. John, New Brunswick, Canada. *Environmental Health Perspectives* 104 (1): 1354–60.

Stoto, M. A. 1983. The Accuracy of Population Projections. *Journal of the American Statistical Association* 78 (381): 13–20.

Tietenberg, T. H. 1980. Transferable Discharge Permits and the Control of Stationary Source Air Pollution: A Survey and Synthesis. *Land Economics* 56 (4): 391–416.

Tol, R. S. J. 2005. The Marginal Damage Costs of Carbon Dioxide Emissions: An Assessment of the Uncertainties. *Energy Policy* 33 (16): 2064–74.

Tong, D. Q., and D. L. Mauzerall. 2006. Spatial Variability of Summertime Tropospheric Ozone over the Continental United States: Implications of an Evaluation of the CMAQ Model. *Atmospheric Environment* 40:3041–56.

Tong, Daniel Q., Nicholas Z. Muller, Denise L. Mauzerall, and Robert O. Mendelsohn. 2006. Integrated Assessment of the Spatial Variability of Ozone Impacts from Emissions of Nitrogen Oxides. *Environmental Science and Technology* 40:1395–1400.

Turner, D. B. 1994. *Workbook of Atmospheric Dispersion Estimates: An Introduction to Dispersion Modeling.* 2nd ed. Ann Arbor, MI: Lewis Publishers.

U.S. Bureau of Economic Analysis (Department of Commerce). 2009. *Industry Economic Accounts.* http://www.bea.gov/industry/iotables/table_list.cfm?anon=69672.

U.S. Census Bureau. 2000. *Census of Population and Housing.* Washington, DC: U.S. Census Bureau. http://www.census.gov/popest/data/historical/2000s/vintage_2002/county.html

U.S. Department of Agriculture. 2002. *Census of Agriculture.* Washington, DC: U.S. Department of Agriculture.

U.S. Department of Agriculture (U.S. Forest Service). 2008. *Forest Inventory Data Online* http://fia.fs.fed.us/tools-data/.

U.S. Department of Energy. 1992. *Commercial Buildings Energy Consumption and Expenditures 1989.* DOE/EIA–0318(89). Washington, DC: U.S. Department of Energy.

———.1993. *Household Energy Consumption and Expenditures 1990.* DOE/EIA–0321/1(90). Washington, DC: U.S. Department of Energy.

U.S. Energy Information Administration. 2008. *Independent Statistics and Analysis.* http://www.eia.gov/electricity/data.cfm#elecenv (accessed May 1, 2011).

USEPA (U.S. Environmental Protection Agency). 1997. *The Benefits and Costs of the Clean Air Act: 1970–1990. EPA Report to Congress.* Office of Air and Radiation; Office of Policy. EPA 410–R–99–001, Washington, DC.

———. 1999. *The Benefits and Costs of the Clean Air Act 1990 to 2010. EPA Report to Congress.* Office of Air and Radiation; Office of Policy. EPA–410–R–99–001, Washington, DC.

———. 2004. *Regulatory Impact Analysis of the Final Industrial Boilers and Process Heaters NESHAP: Final Report.* EPA–452/R–04–002, Office of Air Quality Planning and Standards, Washington, DC.

———. 2005. *CMAQ Model Performance Evaluation Report for 2001.* Office of Air Quality Planning and Standards, Emissions Analysis and Monitoring Division, Air Quality Modeling Group, Research Triangle Park, NC. http://epa.gov/scram001/reports/cair_final_cmaq_model_performance_evaluation_2149.pdf.

————. 2006. *National Emissions Inventory 2002*. Office of Air Quality Planning and Standards, Emissions Inventory Group; Emissions, Monitoring, and Analysis Division, Washington, DC.

————. 2007. *Annual Emission Report: Acid Rain Program 2002*. Office of Air and Radiation, Clean Air Markets Division, Washington, DC. http://camddataandmaps.epa.gov/gdm/.

————. 2008. *National Air Pollutant Emission Trends, 1900–1998*. Office of Air Quality Planning and Standards, EPA–454/R–00–002, Research Triangle Park, NC.

————. 2012. http://www.epa.gov/ttn/airs/airsaqs/detaildata/downloadaqsdata.htm

U.S. National Acid Precipitation Assessment Program (NAPAP). 1991a. *1990 Integrated Assessment Report*. Washington, DC: U.S. National Acid Precipitation Assessment Program.

————. 1991b. *Acidic Deposition: State of Science and Technology*. 4 vols. Washington, DC: U.S. National Acid Precipitation Assessment Program.

————. 1991c. Economic Valuation of Changes in Visibility: A State of the Science Assessment for NAPAP. In *Methods for Valuing Acidic Deposition and Air Pollution Effects*. National Acid Precipitation Assessment Program Report 27:. 27-153 to 27-175. Washington, D.C. U.S. National Acid Precipitation Assessment Program.

U.S. National Oceanic and Atmospheric Administration. 2000.

Vardon, Michael, Manfred Lenzen, Stuart Peevor, and Mette Creaser. 2007. Water Accounting in Australia. *Ecological Economics* 61:650–59.

Viscusi, W. Kip, and Joseph E. Aldy. 2003. The Value of a Statistical Life: A Critical Review of Market Estimates throughout the World. *Journal of Risk and Uncertainty* 27 (1): 5–76.

World Bank. 1997. *Expanding the Measure of Wealth: Indicators of Environmentally Sustainable Development*. Washington, DC: World Bank.

About the Authors

Nicholas Z. Muller is assistant professor in the Department of Economics and the environmental studies program at Middlebury College, where he teaches microeconomics, environmental economics, and environmental policy. Dr. Muller's research has been published in the *American Economic Review, Science,* the *Journal of Environmental Economics and Management,* and the *Journal of Policy Analysis and Management,* among other outlets. In addition, he has worked directly with the United Nations Environment Programme and the National Academies of Science. Dr. Muller's research is currently supported by the U.S. Environmental Protection Agency's National Center for Environmental Economics. He received his Ph.D. in environmental economics from the School of Forestry and Environmental Studies at Yale University in 2007, his master's degree in public administration from Indiana University–Bloomington in 2002, and his bachelor's degree with honors from the University of Oregon in 1996.

Robert Mendelsohn, Edwin Weyerhaeuser Davis Professor at Yale University, is a resource economist specializing in valuing the environment. Dr. Mendelsohn began his research career estimating the damage of air pollution emissions from fossil fuel plants using an integrated assessment model. He has recently returned to this topic with Professor Muller. Dr. Mendelsohn has also developed methods to value local hazardous waste pollution, local wildlife populations, recreation areas, oil spills, and non-timber products from tropical forests. Over the last fifteen years, Dr. Mendelsohn has been involved in measuring the impacts from climate change, including adaptation. With Dr. Nordhaus and Dr. Shaw, he developed the Ricardian technique to measure climate impacts to agriculture, which has now been applied in over thirty countries across the world. With Dr. Sohngen, he developed an ecological model of forests combined with a dynamic economic model to predict a path of global timber impacts from climate change. With Dr. Morrison and Dr. Mansur, he developed a model of fuel choice to estimate the impacts of climate change on energy. More recently, Dr. Mendelsohn has completed a set of studies on farm adaptations with colleagues across the world.